GLOBETROTTER™

Trave

C000172282

KRAKOW
AND POLAND

PAUL TINGAY

NEW
HOLLAND

NEW
HOLLAND

★★★ Highly recommended
★★ Recommended
★ See if you can

First edition published in 2009
by New Holland Publishers (UK) Ltd
London • Cape Town • Sydney • Auckland
10 9 8 7 6 5 4 3 2 1

website: www.newhollandpublishers.com

Garfield House, 86 Edgware Road
London W2 2EA, United Kingdom

80 McKenzie Street
Cape Town 8001, South Africa

Unit 1, 66 Gibbes Street,
Chatswood, NSW 2067, Australia

218 Lake Road, Northcote,
Auckland, New Zealand

Distributed in the USA by
The Globe Pequot Press, Connecticut

Publishing Manager: Thea Grobbelaar
DTP Cartographic Manager: Genené Hart
Editor: Thea Grobbelaar
Design and DTP: Nicole Bannister
Cartographer: Reneé Spocter
Picture Researcher: Shavonne Govender
Consultant: Rachel F Freeman
Proofreader: Elizabeth Wilson
Reproduction by Resolution (Cape Town).
Printed and bound by Times Offset (M) Sdn. Bhd.,
Malaysia.

Acknowledgments:
The author would like to thank Caroline Tingay,
Dominik Collenberg, Ann of the Tatras, Patience
Manyora and especially Danuta Piekarz for her
Polish hospitality and invaluable assistance.

Keep us Current
Information in travel guides is apt to change, which is
why we regularly update our guides. We'd be grateful
to receive feedback if you've noted something we
should include in our updates. If you have new
information, please share it with us by writing to the
Publishing Manager, Globetrotter, at the office
nearest to you (addresses on this page). The most
significant contribution to each new edition will
receive a free copy of the updated guide.

CONTENTS

1
Introducing Kraków and Poland

Zurek, the delicious Polish soup, is made from rye flour, sour cream, hard-boiled eggs and sausages. In fact, there is a little of everything in it – rather like Poland.

Kraków, medieval city of kings, covers an area of 327km² (126 sq miles), one-sixth the size of London; its population, at 757,000, is half that of **Warsaw**, today's capital. Situated in the misty Vistula Valley, Kraków is divided by five of that great river's tributaries. The first person to write of Kraków (known as the city of poets) was a Jewish travelling salesman with an Arabic name, Ibrahim ibn Yacub, in AD965. At the turn of the millennium a church was built and Kraków, being somewhat safer from marauding Czechs, replaced Gniezno as King Bolesław the Brave's capital. After being sacked by the Mongol Huns in 1241 Kraków's fortifications were mightily improved with 47 towers, walls up to 9m (30ft) high and huge gates closed at nightfall. In 1364 Kazimierz the Great established a university.

Kraków, like all Poland, has had to face a legion of enemies, but fortunately in World War II was insufficiently strategically sited to attract the predations of Hitler's *Wehrmacht* and Stalin's Red Army. Kraków's 6000 listed historical buildings, 88 palaces, 87 churches and 46 cemeteries have largely been preserved, which is why visiting Kraków is such a delight. There is, however, one terrible scar on its communal memory: 120km (75 miles) to the west is the town of Oświęcim, the Auschwitz-Birkenau death camp where millions were tortured, brutalized and ultimately exterminated by the Nazis. Today it is a place of obligatory pilgrimage for all Polish and Israeli teenagers.

TOP ATTRACTIONS

*** Kraków: Town Market Square, St Mary's Gothic Church.
*** Wawel Hill and old Royal Castle: towering above the Vistula River.
*** Mikolajki and Mazuria Lake District: lonely forests and lakes.
** Gdańsk and Baltic Sea: solidarity and the fight against Communism.
** Zakopane and Tatra Mountains: old wooden houses and snow-bound ski peaks.

Opposite: *Carefully tended gardens fringe the courtyard to Wawel's hill-top cathedral in Kraków.*

FACT FILE

• Kraków is the historical capital of Poland and Warsaw (pronounced 'Vashavah') the modern one.
• Polish is spoken by 99% of Poland's 38.5 million people, with a touch of German, Lithuanian, Czech, Slovak, Romany, Tatar, Russian and Ukrainian for flavour.
• 80% of Poles practise the Catholic religion.
• Clockwise, Poland is surrounded on the map by 450km (280 miles) of Baltic Sea coast in the north, then the Russian enclave of Kaliningrad, then Lithuania, Belarus, Ukraine, Slovakia, the Czech Republic and Germany.
• The difference, they say, between Polish and Russian men is that two Poles will share a bottle of vodka for lunch, whereas the Russians will have a bottle each.
• Before Hitler's death camps, there were 3.3 million Polish Jews. Now there are fewer than 10,000.
• Chicago (USA) has 1 million citizens of Polish descent. Others are in the UK and Eire.

THE LAND

Flanked by Germany in the west, the Baltic Sea in the north, and by six other countries (including Russia) to the east and south, Poland has always been – dangerously – the land in the middle.

Poland consists mainly of low undulating plains. Hence *Polonie*: 'the people of the plains'. This has proved a defence hazard. The Carpathian (including Tatra) and Sudeten mountains define its southern border. It covers an area a third larger than the UK, 312,683km^2 (120,774 sq miles), stretching from the lovely sand dune beaches along its 450km (280-mile) Baltic shore to its snow-capped Tatra (Tatry) mountains in the south. Berlin is only 80km (50 miles) from its border.

Apart from the ancient historical centres in practically every city (some meticulously rebuilt post World War II), Poland's great attractions have always been its **Mazurian Lake District**, the mountainous **Tatras** for skiing and hiking, and the long empty beaches of the **Baltic**.

Kraków (sometimes written 'Cracow' but pronounced 'Krakoof') is the architectural, cultural and historical heart of Poland, a country that, down the centuries, has some-

Right: *The peaceful forested shores of Lake Wigry in northeast Poland near Suwałki.*

how managed to survive the territorial ambitions of its giant neighbours to east and west. In the process the Poles have become an exceptionally tough and resilient people who guard their Slavonic language, their Catholic religion and their ancient cities such as Kraków with a fierce pride.

Plains and Mountains

Poland is, in fact, only flat in the wide grassy plains of the central Wielkopolska (Great Poland) which for many centuries has been Poland's grain belt and source of trading wealth. Poland's tallest mountain, **Mount Rysy** (2499m or 8199ft), is located in the Tatras. Hugging the Tatras is the heavily forested but lower Beskidy range. From there northwards the land descends to Małopolska (Little Poland). In the north towards Olsztyn and Gdańsk there are over 9000 **glacial lakes**, a record in Europe only capped by Finland. The **Vistula (Wisła) River** cuts right through the country south to north. It is 1047km (650 miles) long, roughly the length of the country. All of Poland's rivers drain into the **Baltic Sea**, the second largest being the **Odra (Oder) River** on the German border which ends in a vast shallow lagoon 50km (31 miles) wide near the city of Szczecin or, in German, Stettin.

GREEN STATISTICS

Just over 1% of Poland's land has been set aside as national parks, although another 11% consists of 'landscape' areas. There are 22 national parks. Per person, Poland emits eight tonnes of carbon dioxide annually – 25% that of the largest culprit, the United Arab Emirates, and not as much as 29 other countries. Forty per cent of Poland's 312,683km² (120,774 sq miles) is arable but of this only 0.36% is organic crop land (Austria tops the organic bill with 11.6%). Australia has by far the world's largest number of nature reserves.

There are freeways from Germany and the Czech Republic, but few in Poland other than from Kraków to Dresden, Konin to Poznań, and a good link between the Baltic holiday resorts of Gdańsk, Sopot and Gdynia. More are under construction. Poland has 19,600km (12,171 miles) of railways, more than Spain, Italy or the UK.

Climate

If you enjoy skiing, then winter – especially January through to March – is the time to visit Poland. Otherwise stick to spring, autumn and summer, in that order. Subject to global warming or a new mini ice age, March is usually the start of spring in Poland and even then it can be sunny. Summer rains come during the warm months of June to September and especially in July. It gets misty in November and can be very cold. From December to March there is plenty of snow that can last until early May in the Tatras.

Below: *Poland's southern Tatra mountains bordering Slovakia are ideal for skiing.*

The weather in Poland is what TV forecasters like to call 'variable', mainly because it is subject to two systems: a continental climate from the east (Siberia and central Russia) and a maritime climate from the west (Baltic Sea). It can quickly change from day to day, year to year.

HISTORY IN BRIEF

Millions of years ago, man first emerged from his forest home to walk on the vast plains of East Africa, leaving his footprints in the volcanic ash for posterity. He then gradually migrated north, following and hunting the game as the herds crossed over the then watered grasslands of the Sahara into the land-bridged Middle East.

Half a million years ago the total world population may only have been some 8000 souls. These 'wise men' (*Homo sapiens*), however, increased in numbers and began hunting and gathering foods all over the veld. The breakthrough came in the 'Fertile Crescent' – the areas watered by the Tigris, Euphrates and Nile rivers – 50,000 years ago. Humans were now in possession of fire and had started cultivating the land. Animals were domesticated, decent housing built and mystical rock painting developed.

Horsemen of the Steppe

It did not take long for the first prehistoric or pre-literate farmers of Central Europe, the Linearbandkeramik Culture, to grow crop surpluses, fashion sophisticated weapons and, because of their proximity to domesticated livestock, develop immunity to many diseases. Thus with the Ice Age's great sheets receding from Europe about 11,000 years ago, insatiably curious humans could continue their migrations. There is no such thing as an indigenous people; mankind has always been an immigrant.

Indo-European horsemen were northern Europe's first wave of migrants to the Ukraine, Poland's eastern neighbour some 4000–6000 years ago, then a wasteland of shimmering grass, snow and moving water.

Arrows and Stirrups

Man has seldom been a peaceful creature. The story of Europe over the last few thousand years – as the Poles inevitably caught in the middle are only too aware – has been one of continual tribal warfare which really only ended with the formation of the UN in 1945, and later the EU. Stirrups for their horses, bows and arrows, and horse-drawn war chariots some 3500 years ago enabled

HISTORICAL CALENDAR

6000–4000BC Indo-European horsemen appear on the Plains of Poland.

AD500 Fall of the Europe-wide empire of ancient Rome and start of the so-called Dark Ages (i.e. post-classical Rome); Slav-speaking tribes (Polonians or 'people of the plains') migrate into modern Poland.

750–1250 Roman Catholicism conquers and converts most of Europe.

965 First recorded Polish history. Six Polanie tribes are united under warlord Mieszko I, Piast duke, who converts to Catholicism as a politically protective measure.

992 Mieszko unites his tribal area into Wielkopolska or Great Poland, roughly today's Poland (225,000km² or 87,000 sq miles). Gniezno becomes the capital of Poland.

1038 Kraków becomes Poland's capital; here 37 coronations took place and all but two Polish kings are buried.

1241 Kraków is razed by the Tatars (or Mongols or Huns)

under Ogodei Khan. The Mongol empire stretches from Kraków to Karyo (Korea), a distance of nearly 10,000km (6000 miles); capital: Karakorum.

700–1300 Middle Ages (between classical Rome and the Renaissance); watermill, spinning wheel and soap invented. Cathedrals built. Crusades.

1333–70 Kazimierz the Great. He made Poland rich and protected the Jews.

1300–1500 One third of Europe's population perishes in repeated plagues. Agricultural Revolution and migration to the cities.

1473–1543 Mikołaj Kopernik (Copernicus) proves the theory that the earth revolves around the sun and not vice versa.

1673 Jan Sobieski defeats rampaging Ottoman Turks at Battle of Chocim and raises their siege of Vienna in 1683.

1772–95 Partition of Poland by Russia, Austria and Prussia. Poland loses most of its

inhabitants and territory and de facto ceases to exit.

1730–1900 Industrial Revolution: the age of railways, canals, Nobel's dynamite, telephone, light bulb, camera, sewing machine, 'white collar' workers.

1810–49 Life of Frédéric Chopin (in Polish Fryderyk Szopen), Polish composer.

1867–1934 Maria Skłodowska (Marie Curie) discovers radium and polonium. First woman (and double) Nobel winner.

1918 Marshal Józef Piłsudski declares Poland's independence and defeats Soviets in battle.

1939–45 World War II, and Poland is attacked by both Hitler and Stalin; some 25% of Poles killed.

1978 Karol Wojtyła becomes Pope John Paul II, the first non-Italian pope since 1522.

1990 Solidarity, Gdańsk and the shipyard unions force Poland's freedom from communism.

1999 Poland joins Nato.

2004 Poland joins the EU.

migrating Indo-Europeans to replace – actually wipe out – those who had journeyed before, grabbing Poland's amber, grain, ore and, as a *divertissement du guerre*, women. The oldest tribes in Europe are now the **Celts** (Ireland, Wales), the **Basque** (Spain) and the 250,000 **Romany** pejoratively called gypsies in the mistaken belief that they originated in Egypt (they came from India).

Anatolia (Turkey) and the Ukraine, which stretches for 1300km (800 miles) east of Poland, were the twin birthplaces of Indo-European languages which include Latin, Greek and the Indian Sanskrit. Poles speak what is called a West-Slavonic Indo-European variant.

Plain Folk

Creeping around eerie forests armed with spears and being gored by boars is the depiction of the Dark Ages (AD500–1000), so called by a later generation bemoaning the demise of classical Rome. They soon became less dark once **Charlemagne** founded the **Holy Roman Empire** and encouraged all to read, even if he couldn't himself, thus inspiring everyone to begin building those great soaring Gothic churches, of which St Mary's in Kraków is a particularly beautiful example.

Roman or **Catholic Christianity** emerged as the single most powerful unifying force among the tribes of Europe after the demise of ancient Rome. The word 'Slav' actually derives from the Christian epithet for a 'pagan' or someone who could justifiably be enslaved. Slav tribes migrated from the southeast onto the grassy lowlands or Steppe some 1400 years ago, choosing rivers such as the Vistula (Wisła) along which to live.

Polonians

The Poles came to be known as the Polonians, the people of the open fields or plains. Their language was a powerful cohesive factor, much more so than with the German tribes to the south. There was a small group of six Polish-speaking *Polanie* tribes living near the River Warta, not far from today's historic towns of Poznań and Gniezno. United under the semimythical Piast chieftains, they came to be called **Polska**. The birth of the nation was consolidated in 965 by **Duke Mieszko I** who married the Duke of Bohemia's daughter and also made a politically astute conversion to catholicism, thus guaranteeing Papal and Holy Roman Empire protection. Kraków became the capital of Poland in 1038.

Middle Ages

Practically every town in Poland has a *Stare Miasto*, an old medieval town, the most

Below: *Ojców National Park near Kraków has many old castles built by King Kazimierz the Great.*

BURNING GOLD

The mythical Mines of King Solomon, with which he supposedly wooed the Queen of Sheba, did not reveal any gold. Neither did many of man's golden quests, other than the miles-deep mine shafts of South Africa which produce 297 tonnes a year. **Michał Sędziwój** (or Sędzimir or even Sondivogius) was born in Łukowica in the foothills of the Tatra Mountains in 1566. Michał was a man of many talents: secretary to the king, diplomat and scholar. Some maintain he even identified oxygen. He also claimed he had discovered the philosopher's stone, the elixir that turned rock into gold – every scientist's dream-wish of the time. He was imprisoned in Germany for his impertinence.

colourful and largest being that of Kraków. St Mary's lovely church there was begun in AD1000. Renaissance Italians invented the expression 'the Middle Ages' to cover the centuries between the fall of their beloved Rome and the emergence of scholarship, art, science, and new world discoveries of their own born-again era. To them, the new cathedrals that had blossomed throughout Europe were 'Gothic' – creations of the dreadful civilization-destroying Goths or Germans or even Poles.

Islam, meanwhile, fired by the prophet Mohammed's exquisitely poetic Qur'an, had conquered the Middle East. Catholic Christians, cross in one hand, sword in the other, were determined to rescue the Holy Places where Jesus had lived, so they set out on a series of crusades. Those along the route had their castles ruined, cities razed and women raped.

The medieval invention of the water mill, the expansion of the textile industry through the spinning wheel, the use of soap, iron-casting techniques and the Chinese invention of gunpowder all helped to change European and also Polish society. Devotion to the saints, their relics, and to Mary, mother of Jesus, expanded enormously. However, poor harvests created homeless people. And then came bubonic plague.

The **Black Death** or Plague was not new to Europe. Up to 30 million died from the flea-and-rat-borne disease that spread through Europe as the Roman Empire disintegrated. The plague may well have been one of the unsung causes that precipitated the fracture of Roman hegemony into Europe's dozens of tribal and fratricidal nation states. Right from the start the Poles had to defend themselves against the

CRACOVIA

encroachment of Germans from the west, Prussians from the north and both Bohemians and Hungarians from the south. (The Poles, of course, were not averse to the occasional landgrab themselves.)

A new and far worse threat came in 1241 when Kraków was attacked by the ferocious horsemen of **Ogodei Khan**, the son of **Chinggis (Genghis) Khan**. Three times the Tatars came to kill and plunder. With them from the Gobi Desert they brought the plague. Subsequently – between 1300 and 1500 – a third of Europe's population perished.

Religion Rules

Kazimierz III (the Great) died in 1370. During his 37-year reign he pulled the country together, built cities and founded a school in Kraków in 1364 that later became a university and the most sophisticated intellectual centre in Europe.

Politics, religion, money and the delights of the flesh have occupied the Poles as much as any people. But in Poland, come the 16th century, religious argument always seemed more important. Revolutionary reformer **Martin Luther** of Germany dramatically arrived on the scene, after which nationalism, politics, economics, social justice, religious schism and war became thoroughly intertwined. The birth of **Protestantism** (a more direct relationship with Jesus, correct reading of the Bible and a return to an older and purer Christianity) and the Catholic Church's reaction to it were to trouble Europe for the next four centuries.

This was also the era when Poland's **Mikołaj Kopernik**, or **Nicolaus Copernicus** (1473–1543), confirmed that the earth revolves around the sun, thus launching modern astronomy. **Blaise Pascal** invented the first adding machine, **Isaac Newton** calculus; and the new printing presses launched propaganda, pornography and, strangely, a new piety. The Portuguese invented the caravel ship, leading to exploration and discovery of what to Europe was a brave New World. And everyone was using new cannons and eastern gunpowder in fighting religious wars, the worst of which was the Europe-wide **Thirty Years War**

Opposite: *This 1493 print of medieval Kraków is the earliest known view of the city.*

Above: *Mikołaj Kopernik, or Copernicus, was an architect, lawyer, doctor, soldier, priest and astronomer from Toruń.*

of 1618–48). Disaster replaced prosperity as the war put an end to Catholic supremacy in Europe and killed off 30% of the continent's population.

Poland in Decline

Commander **Jan Sobieski** saved Poland from the predatory Ottoman Turks, firstly at the battle of Chocim in 1673 (for which a grateful nation made him king) and ten years later, in 1683, his cavalry trounced them again, thus rescuing the Holy Roman Empire and its capital, Vienna.

But the good times did not last. Successor to Sobieski was **Augustus the Strong** (he fathered 300 children). In fact, he was weak. Brandenburg-Prussia and the Swedes all but annihilated Poland during the reign of this inept king. The economy declined steadily from 1648–1795. The Vistula grain trade collapsed, the nobles spent most of their time fighting each other, while plague, poverty and agricultural enclosures devastated the people.

Around this time potatoes and sugar were introduced from the Americas. Thomas Malthus wrote his *Essay on the Principle of Population* and soon it was the age of Voltaire, Rousseau, Adam Smith and Enlightenment. Gilt-adorned Baroque came into vogue, as did Goethe's romanticism. In Poland, **Gabriel Daniel Fahrenheit** invented the mercury thermometer. Strangely, it was also around this time that burning witches at the stake became increasingly common.

Partition

In 1772 came the disastrous **First Partition of Poland** by Russia, Austria and Prussia. Poland lost a third of its territory and 50% of its inhabitants.

Then in 1793 came the second landgrab. Russia took what was left of Lithuania and most of the western Ukraine. Prussia took Gdańsk and beautiful medieval

Toruń plus Greater Poland. This time Poland lost 4.1 million of its inhabitants.

Two years later, in 1795, 3.2 million inhabitants (and their lands, including Warsaw) went to Russia and Prussia, while Austria took the Kraków area. Poland fought back, of course, against this attack. War General **Tadeusz Kościuszko** won a memorable victory with his scythe-wielding peasants at Racławice, some 40km (25 miles) northeast of Kraków. But to no avail. Even the name, Poland, was abolished.

French Revolution

The king of England (Charles I) lost his head in 1649, the American colonies won their independence in 1783, and the *citoyens* of Paris stormed the Bastille on 14 July 1789. Power to the people – well, the well-connected ones. For 22 years Europe was in turmoil as **Napoleon** sought to anchor the French Revolution throughout Europe.

Bonaparte saw Poland as an ally. In 1807 the Duchy of Warsaw's Polish Commander, **Józef Pontiatowski**, threw in his lot with the daring Corsican warlord, and by 1812 the 'Polish War' won back for Poland the disputed Lithuanian lands. But it was too little, too late. Napoleon was retreating from his ill-fated winter offensive in Moscow, and Pontiatowski, in romantic Polish fashion, led his troops in a suicidal last stand against the Russians and Prussians at Napoleon's defeat in 1813 in Leipzig, Germany. Thereafter, **Warsaw** was more or less dismissed as the '**Congress Kingdom**' (after the 1814–15 Congress of Vienna which divided up the post-Napoleonic spoils).

Industrial Revolution

Britain's Industrial Revolution of the 18th century spread to Europe in the 19th: railways, canals, communal farming, the telegraph, Colt revolvers, Singer sewing machines (1870), the first oil well (1859), Mackintosh raincoats, Nobel's dynamite, Otis's elevator, mass circulation newspapers,

---

POLAND'S BEST

Composer: Frédéric Chopin (1810–49)
Freedom fighter: Józef Piłsudski (1867–1935)
Nobel prize-winning novelist: Władysław Reymont (1868–1925)
Poet, dramatist: Stanisław Wyspiański (1869–1907)
Physicist, double Nobel prize winner: Maria Skłodowska (Marie Curie, 1867–1934)
Musician: Ignacy Paderewski (1860–1941)
Writer: Józef Konrad Korzeniowski (1857–1924)
Explorer: Ignacy Domeyko (1802–89)
Astronomer: Jan Śniadecki (1756–1830)
Painter: Jan Matejko (1839–93)
Poet: Adam Mickiewicz (1798–1855)

Below: *The Polish flag in two broad panels of red and white. The papal flag in yellow and white is also popular.*

HITLER

'Uncontrolled madness ... unique in history' is how Italian Auschwitz survivor and famed writer Primo Levi answers the question as to why the Nazis hated the Jews. Hitler convinced himself that he was the Hero, the Super-man redeemer of Germany, prophesied by Nietzsche. What is it that drives tyrants? In Hitler's case, it's possible that his fits of rage, blame, depression, wild decisions and violence can in part be attributed to bipolar disorder at a time when there was no medication for the disease, or to neuro-syphilis, curable by penicillin only available in the medical armoury of his Anglo-American enemies.

Gillette's safety razor (1895), Remington's typewriter (1874), telephones, Edison's light bulb, Dunlop pneumatic tyres and the Kodak camera (1888), to name just a few. This was the era of Charles Dickens, Vincent van Gogh, Manet, the first skyscraper, music halls, sports spectacles, Louis Pasteur's medical breakthroughs, Sigmund Freud's psychoanalysis and Poland's favourite daughter, double Noble prize winner **Maria Skłodowska (Marie Curie)** from Warsaw, who discovered polonium and radium. Department stores, 'big' business, 'white collar' workers and mass consumerism came into vogue.

This was the era when Poland struggled to rid itself of 'The Partitions'. The Russians crushed an uprising in 1830–31, leading to mass immigration to the USA. Friedrich Engels (the communist philosopher) maintained that Poland's liberation was the most important objective of the workers of the world. In 1863–64 there was another insurrection, again viciously crushed by Russia, into which Poland was incorporated as 'Vistulaland'.

Right: *Grim watchtowers at Auschwitz-Birkenau Nazi death camp where millions of Jews lost their lives in the gas chambers.*

Modern Times

Competing European nationalisms fed by inordinate industrial wealth led in 1914 to **World War I**. Millions perished in the mud and hellfire of Flanders. At its conclusion in 1918, a revenge-obsessed France more or less ensured the rise of Hitler.

On 11 November 1918 Marshal **Józef Piłsudski** took command of Warsaw and declared Poland an independent state under a Regency Council, with famed concert pianist **Ignacy Jan Paderewski** as prime minister. Gdańsk (or Danzig) remained on its own as a city-state (its population at the time was still mainly German), and Poland got its portion of the territorial share-out.

Poland Since World War II

But having **Stalin** to the east and **Hitler** to the west was hardly conducive to peace of mind. Non-aggression pacts with Russia and Germany were not worth the paper they were written on, as both regarded Poland as feeding ground for their territorial ambitions. On 1 September 1939 Hitler invaded Poland, launching **World War II**. Seventeen days later it was Stalin's turn to attack Poland. The Poles fought courageously – even mounting a cavalry charge and many joining the RAF – for five weeks, but it was hopeless.

Twenty-five per cent of Poles were killed between 1939 and 1945 and the country's peoples were shunted about en masse according to the ethnic cleansing whims of both Stalin and Hitler. In 1944–45, America (for the second time in 25 years) rescued and freed Europe.

The Polish people rose up in strikes against the Soviets and their own Polish puppets in 1956, 1970, 1971, 1976, 1980, 1981 and 1988. With the support of the Catholic Church and especially their very own **Pope John Paul II**, Poland finally won its freedom in 1989, the first Communist country in Eastern Europe to do so since World War II.

Poland held its first free elections in 1991. Gdańsk Trade Union Solidarity leader **Lech Wałęsa** became president. In 1993 the last of 60,000 Soviet troops quit Poland. In 1999 Poland joined **NATO**, supported the West in its war against Saddam Hussein in Iraq, and joined the **EU** in May 2004.

NATION'S HERO

Father of the modern Polish nation, **Józef Piłsudski**, having fought against Tsarist hegemony, declared Poland independent (which it had not been for 123 years) on 11 November 1918, Poppy Day. He soon began a military campaign to reclaim Polish eastern territories lost in the landgrab 'Partitions' of the 18th century. By mid-1920, however, the Bolsheviks were at Warsaw's door. But in the 'Miracle on the Wisła' Marshall Piłsudski outmanoeuvred and thoroughly defeated the Soviets, thus, albeit indirectly, saving Germany from the Red Peril. He is buried in the crypt of Kraków's hilltop Wawel Cathedral among the kings of Poland.

Right: *Warsaw is the only city in Poland to have a Metro, begun in 1983.*

GOVERNMENT AND ECONOMY

Poland is a parliamentary democracy in which the ultra-conservative **Law and Justice Party** lost its majority in elections in October 2007 to the pro-business **Civic Platform Party** (PO) led by **Donald Tusk** (pronounced 'Toosk'), which is more pro-EU than the President-and-former-Prime-Minister-twins combination, the **Kaczyński brothers**, whom Poland's vibrant press loved to lampoon. The twins were bent on hunting down former communists who, like many Nazis in Germany and Austria, quietly shrank away into the mists of 'we did not know'.

The Law and Justice Party sees itself as the post-Solidarity 'morally pure Poland', its enemies liberal and 'spoiled'. The Civic Platform Party will have to go some way to mend fences with Germany and the EU whom Poland – as independent-minded as ever – chose on occasion to upset.

Poland was the only EU country to try and block Europe's 2007 anti-death penalty day. (Being fiercely Catholic, it wanted it to include an anti-abortion and anti-euthanasia clause.) **Aleksander Kwaśiewski** and **Lech Kaczyński** continue to contend for the presidency.

EU: Pros and Cons

Economically, Poland could well be the next 'Tiger' or 'Wild Geese' leader in central Europe. Its economy has over the past few years been growing at 5%. Living standards (and many prices) are fast catching up with those of the European Union, but a lot of young Poles still live with their parents, rents being high. Poland's Gross Domestic Product (the total value of all goods and services produced in Poland during one year) stands at US$303 billion, with services accounting for 64% of this, industry 31% and agriculture 5%. Some 37.2% of the country's GDP comes from exports. Foreign Direct Investment (FDI) combined with a highly skilled workforce are playing a key role in development.

Income per head is roughly US$7880 and rising. Unemployment is steadily decreasing, currently standing at 12%. Principal exports are hi-tech machinery, transport equipment and manufactured goods (cars, information technology, electronics). Germany is Poland's main export destination (neighbours nearly always are), accounting for some 28.1% of the total. Poland's reserves stand at over US$2 billion. Poland's economy in GDP terms is slightly lower than Austria's, considerably larger than the Czech Republic's and Hungary's, and 40% that of Russia.

CLANKETY-CLANK

In the 1950s Kraków's Market Square was closed off to the much loved but noisy horse-drawn trams that had made their debut in October 1882. Tram ticket earnings on that first day were added to the Adam Mickiewicz monument fund. Adam was a Jewish-descended 19th-century romantic patriotic writer. There are 200 trams in Kraków with 434 cars and they come in all colours and with dazzling advertisements.

Below: *Poland, and especially Gdańsk, is famous for its amber jewellery crafted from Ice-Age tree resin.*

Economic Statistics

Poland supplies 0.78% of world exports, higher than Turkey, Israel or Portugal. Its balance of payments deficit is half that of South Africa. Its expatriate workers remit to Poland some US$3.5 billion annually. A Big Mac costs US$2.29 in Poland, cheaper than in Japan or Pakistan. Poland's foreign debt stands at US$98.8 bil-

MOBILE PHONES

Nervous? Need something to do? Take out your mobile phone. Mobiles have revolutionized Polish life. At airports, on planes, buses, in parks, restaurants, walking down the street, everyone is chatting, sending vital messages. The tiny machines come in every shape, colour and giddy function. A mobile in your handbag is a status symbol, worn on your belt, a fashion statement. Teenagers live, love and expire on them. Mobiles and the less intrusive iPods are the ultimate boulevardier gadget. The phones announce their presence with a rollcall blast whose urgency takes precedence over every other exigency. Alexander Graham Bell invented the telephone in 1876. He may now be turning over a missed call in his grave.

lion, half that of Brazil. Poland's industrial output is higher than that of Belgium, Ireland or Argentina. Poland produces copper, (more than Zambia), lead, silver (6th largest producer after Chile), and coal (the world's 8th largest producer, and the source of 94.1% of its own power). Kraków gets 9 million visitors annually, over 2 million of whom are foreigners.

THE PEOPLE

A visitor enters an ancient Polish church hesitantly. She asks the elderly attendant collecting the entrance fee if she can take photographs. Grinning, he holds one hand over his eyes and waves her through: typical Polish devil-may-care humour. The Poles have seen and lived through everything: war, invasion, contempt, slaughter, obliteration, even the death camps of Hitler in which so many of them died 60 years ago.

In the course of a thousand years caught between giant and aggressive neighbours, they have withstood the Nazis, Soviets, Lithuanians, Prussians, Ukrainians, Austro-Hungarians, betrayal and untold hardship. But somehow they, their culture, their Catholic religion, language and pride have survived it all. The Poles are a very experienced, worldly-wise, individualistic and tough people.

You often feel the people of Poland have a tongue-in-cheek attitude towards the rest of the world. Asked to a party: 'Shall I bring a bottle?' 'No, just girls,' is the reply. You will see people praying intensely in church portals. Many young men have shaven heads, others are solemn. Nuns are everywhere, as are the sirens of police cars. Men wear black suits at weddings while blonde and bright red hair are the favourite dyes for ladies, although blue is another dazzling option. A priest stops to give his lunchtime chocolate bar to a cripple at St Mary's Church portal. 'Shall I bring the check?' asks a waitress in perfect American. A junkie asks for a cigarette. 'Phew,' he says when you shake your head. Old men in Kraków's Planty Park do not look up from their game of cards beneath the trees. An old lady, bent and head-scarfed, collects chestnuts for supper. The minimum monthly wage is 800zł (US$289).

Poland has a population of 38.5 million people – slightly fewer than Argentina and slightly more than Tanzania. There are 13.6 million households in Poland and – per 100 people – 75 mobile telephones, 19 computers and 31 telephone lines. There are 2.5 medical doctors per 1000 Poles; 97% of children go to secondary school and 50% to university. Poland's fertility rate is only 1.2 and unemployment is relatively high but decreasing. Poland's Human Development index (income, education and life expectancy) stands at a high 86.2.

Some Statistics

Poland is the world's ninth-highest consumer of both coffee and cocoa. The country has won Nobel prizes in chemistry and physics, plus three for literature, and also 66 Olympic gold medals from 1896–2008. Poland's lakes, Baltic shores, skiing in the Tatra Mountains and above all its many magnificent medieval cities attract 15.2 million visitors a year at last count. Eleven per cent of Poland is protected for its stunning scenery, birds and wildlife. Beware: Poles love their vodka (66.2 litres consumed per person per year), and on occasion even drop a tiny glass of it into a glass of beer (which costs half that in an English pub). Everybody seems to smoke (prices: one-fifth that of London). The prison population is higher than that of the UK, Germany or Pakistan.

Language

Polish is a gravel and spit language with 'lots of zedz'. Its alphabet has enough diacritics (marks above or below characters) to rival Hungarian. It even more difficult to learn than English. Latin was the language of Poland

---

MY YIDDISHER MAMA

Yiddish, the former language of European and Polish Jews, is a dialect of High German with Slavonic, Hebrew and Romance (Italian, French) words thrown in for spice. It developed in Central and Eastern Europe during the so-called Middle Ages. It is a colourful vernacular language. In Yiddish, cow's feet in jelly is known as *ptsha*, while the curse of curses is: *zolst farliren aleh tseyner achitz eynm, un dos zol dir vey ton*. This translates as 'hope you lose all your teeth except the one that stays and aches'. The word for 'toe' in Yiddish is *finger*. The Yiddish written alphabet is the Hebrew of Biblical times, and also of today's Israel. Hitler tried very hard to extinguish everything Jewish. Fortunately, he failed.

Opposite: *Traditional dress is worn on festive occasions in the Zakopane area of the Tatra Mountains.*

MAY I HAVE A WORD?

Stare miasto: Old town
Ulica: Street
Kościół: Church
Rynek: Old Town Square
Puszcza: Forest
Pokoje: Rooms
Dzień dobry: Good morning
Dziękuję: Thank you
Prosze: Please (also means 'you're welcome')
Dobrze: OK, fine, good, super
Panowie & Panie: Men's & women's toilets

An entrance is *Wejście* and (confusingly) an exit is *Wyjście.*

in medieval times. Visually fearsome as it is, with its sequences of consonants, it is in fact melodious and can at times sound as bubbly as Italian.

As **tourism** begins to play an increasingly important role in Poland, so English – at least in the cities – is slowly becoming more common, albeit not among taxi drivers and at railway offices. There seem to be English-language schools everywhere. Few people speak English the deeper you venture into the countryside, but sign language always suffices. One visitor, worried that he had boarded the wrong train from Lublin to Kraków, asked if this was the Kraków train. The other passenger looked worried, took out pen and paper, drew a child's picture of a train with eight carriages and wrote 'Kraków' on the first four and 'Warsaw' on the last four. The visitor thanked his new-found artist friend and rapidly went forward.

If you look like a foreigner, most Poles will automatically speak to you in German or even English, or perhaps Russian in the east, as a legacy of the communist era and Russian trade-tourism. German language proficiency comes from the fact that 53% of tourists are German, combined with Poland's long heritage of pre-World War II territorial occupation and population swapping. French is occasionally heard in academic bookshops.

Polish **Kashubian dialect** is spoken by the older generation in the remote area that stretches 100km (60 miles) southwest of Gdańsk. It is an ancient Pomeranian language incorporating some German.

Religion

Karl Marx once wrote that religion was the opiate of the masses – a trifle cynical considering the world's much more fatal addiction to his communism in Russia and China.

Judaism, Islam and Christianity have always intermingled in war, peace, repression and bigotry. Their adherents have killed each other endlessly. But ironically these three great religions have much in common: they all originated in the deserts of the Middle East; they all look upon Abraham as the founding prophet; they all believe in the one God, Jahweh, Allah; and they all put great score by the holy written word: Bible, Torah, Qur'an. And finally they are all, rather quaintly, male-dominated.

Catholic Christianity, the religion of nearly everyone in Poland, is an offshoot of Judaism. Jesus was a Jew, who came to fulfil the ancient prophecies of the Desert Fathers. Catholics believe Jesus was the man-God who, by his compassionate martyrdom, redeemed humanity from what

they perceived to be original sin. Over the centuries, Catholicism tied itself to imperial Rome's hegemony and developed into a wealthy and powerful worldwide bureaucracy of pope, cardinals and priests, an institution somewhat removed from the poor and humble origins of Jesus's teachings. There is truth in the saying, no doubt, that while God invented spirituality, humans invented religion.

Above: *The 17th century saw a profusion of Baroque redecoration in Polish churches.*

Christendom Splits

About 1000 years ago Christendom split into two: **Roman Catholic** to the west, **Byzantine Orthodox** to the east. Poland has always been the front line between western Roman Catholicism and Eastern Orthodox, but only 1% of Poles along its eastern borders are today Orthodox and even fewer are Uniate, or Greek Catholic. There are only a handful of mosques in Poland and, with the elimination of most Jews by the Nazis, only a few synagogues. There is also the occasional Lutheran Church, such as the lovely Parafia Evangelicko – Augusburska ŚW Trójcy in the Lake District of Mikołajki.

Poland is possibly the only country in which one religion is as powerful as for example Islam is in Saudi Arabia. Over 80% of Poles are not only Catholic but actually practise their faith. On a Sunday there are up to nine

POLAND'S POPE

On 2 April 2005, the great bell of Kraków Cathedral rang out for the first time in 26 years. Karol Wojtyła, Poland's own Pope John Paul II, had died. Polish cities practically closed down. He was so loved by the people. He lost his mother when he was nine, his elder brother when he was 12, and his father at 21. He was highly influential in eradicating communism in Poland and subsequently the Soviet Union. He was the youngest pope of the century, the third longest serving in history, and his travels took him around the world 27 times.

crowded masses at any given church. Visitors to churches like medieval St Mary's in Kraków are directed to separate (fee-paying) entrances in order to grant peace and quiet to the praying faithful. Produce a camera without your paparazzi label, however, and the church police will descend on you like a thunderbolt from the Vatican.

Architecture

Poland is a country whose beauty is unsurpassed, especially in autumn with its sun-dappled forests. The first dwellings were made of wood and, although there are many reproduction open-air wooden village museums, the only example of early pre-Slav wooden structures (700BC) is the fortified village of **Biskupin** near Gniezno in the middle of the country.

Romanesque (800–1250) squat pointed-hat churches were the first stone structures. **Gothic** (1300–1500) featured soaring cathedrals, while the **Renaissance** (1500–1650) specialized in interior decoration. **Baroque** (1650–1750) was followed by **Rococo** (1780–1800) a sort of over-the-top Baroque. These were the main European styles, prior to skyscrapers and the steel and glass of modern times. Naturally, imitations of all styles – neo-Gothic, neo-Renaissance – were popular, particularly neo-Roman and Greek classical. Soviet Socialist Realism architecture is reflected in the huge **Palace of Culture and Science** in Warsaw, a sandstone confection of exquisitely ugly inspiration. Like the Empire State Building, its 'neo-brutalist' presence dominates the city.

Many towns, especially the old town centres, were brilliantly reconstructed after World War II. Poland's cities, not having access to American Marshall

Plan funds, however, are often ringed by blocks of soulless dominoes hastily built on platforms of concrete. In the cities there are usually glitzy new overdesigned Galerias or shopping malls, while in the countryside are Monopoly-game double-storey red-roofed houses and, in the south, gorgeous traditional wooden homes.

Art and Sculpture
One woman's painting is another woman's poison. Poland is not universally known for great masters – no Leonardo da Vinci, Rembrandt, Gainsborough or Van Gogh – but the painted vaulted interior of **St Mary's in Kraków** will take your breath away. Wooden carved altarpieces reached a climax of intricate design and storytelling in medieval times. In fact, the interior of a church was often specifically decorated to educate and tell the Christian story to worshippers who could not read or write. Veit Stoss's (Wit Stwosz in Polish) masterpiece in Kraków's St Mary's comes to mind. The Renaissance period concentrated on church chapels and tomb design of which **Wawel Cathedral** is a lovely example.

The 19th century saw the horse paintings of **Piotr Michałowski** (1800–55), the grand patriotic canvases of **Jan Matejko** (1838–93), the Impressionist **Olga Boznańska** (1865–1940), and several Jugendstil or Art Nouveau artists including the young **Stanisław Wyspiański** (1869–1907). The most gifted was **Stanisław Ignacy Witkiewicz** (1885–1939), also known as Witkacy, the much acclaimed (if slightly odd) Renaissance Man of his generation. Poster art from Poland is internationally recognized.

Film and TV
Katyń is Poland's most recent and absorbing film, based on the Soviet murder of over 8000 Polish officers and intelligentsia in World War II. (After having been kept as POWs for a long period of time, they were rounded up in a forest clearing and machine-gunned.)

Piotr Lebiesdziński built a movie camera in 1893, two years before 'flicks' became the craze. The first entirely Polish film was made in 1908, while pre-World War II, **Pola Negri** caused an international splash as an actress.

THREE LITTLE PIGS

The nasty old wolf may well have been able to blow houses down, but he would have had great difficulty in doing so to the wooden houses and churches that used to be all over Poland and are now often gathered together or reconstructed in look-alike wooden villages called *Skansens* – a Scandinavian word meaning 'open-air ethnographic museums'. The earliest wooden fortified village in Poland is the Lusatian or Serb-speaking Biskupin, 80km (50 miles) northeast of Poznań in central Poland. It dates from 550BC. Even the shingles are made of wood. There are over 500 open-air *skansen* museums worldwide. Poland's first was built in 1906 near Gdańsk.

Opposite: *Kraków's Słowacki Theatre, brilliantly lit at night, has an eclectic architectural style.*

SHOPPING

Look for amber, Goldwasser and Kashubian folk art (e.g. embroidered clothes and table cloths) in **Gdańsk**. In **Toruń** you'll find gingerbread cookies in the shape of Copernicus, and in **Poznań** any of Henryk Sienkiewicz's (Nobel Laureate) books, e.g. *Fire in the Steppe, Quo Vadis*. Also in Poznań are *rogale świętomarcińskie* – delicious croissant-like pastries. **Warsaw** is a good place for Polish folk music and coffee-table books. Quite a few bookshops have a foreign (English) section; try the Empik chain. In the **Lake District** the amber jewellery is worth investigating, as is the honey. There are second-hand books on the Old Town Square in **Olsztyn** and the occasional freehand sketch artist of historical buildings. In **Lublin** you'll find postcards of the Castle (chapel) and the many other historic buildings, and also porcelain thimbles with Lublin or Poland on them. The market below the castle walls has almost everything: leather coats, multicoloured bras and switchblades. In the **Tatra Mountains** region you'll find ladies' embroidered tops, men's leather waistcoats, black broad-brimmed cardinals' hats, and thick knitted jerseys. You can also buy local biscuits as well as wooden miniatures of mountain chalets and wooden fretted carvings. For shopping in **Kraków**, *see* page 68.

Wanda Jakubowska, a survivor of Auschwitz, made a powerful documentary of her experiences in the camps. In the 1960s **Roman Polanski** made *Rosemary's Baby* and *Chinatown*. **Janusz Kaminski** (Polish cinematographer) received Oscars for Spielberg's *Schindler's List* and *Saving Private Ryan*. **Adam Holender** was the cinematographer in *Midnight Cowboy*, as was **Andrzej Sekuta** in *Pulp Fiction*. The most successful Polish film was **Jersy Hoffman**'s 1999 adaptation of **Henryk Sienkiewicz**'s patriotic novel *With Fire and Sword*.

There are multi-screen movie complexes in all Polish cities, while local Polish TV has just as many soaps and 'Let's come dancing' cerebral challenges as other countries. Only the occasional private station broadcasts news headlines in English. You can nearly always find a classical music channel among the plethora of Polish pop. Rock'n'roll oldies are much loved – possibly a reaction to the old communist days. Poland has more satellite dishes than anywhere in Europe except the UK and France. Irish pubs in Poland broadcast rugby, a popular sport in the country.

Music Maestro

Poland is the land of the violin – and **folk music**. Buskers are particularly animated on the streets of Poland's cities, ranging from a little Roma boy in Kraków (and his sad-eyed dog) playing the squash-box, to a grey-ponytailed concerto-standard violinist reluctant to be photographed in Lublin.

Benedictine monks and their sublime Gregorian plainchant in Latin were the early 11th-century musicians. Poland's first recognized composer was **Wincenty of Kielce** (1200–1261) who wrote the universally loved Polish hymn, *Gaude Mater Polonia*.

Frédéric Chopin (1810–49) revolutionalized Polish music by adapting the polonaise and mazurka, folk tunes of central Poland, into his evocatively romantic music. Country dance music also inspired **Stanisław Moniuszko** (1819–72), the creator of Polish opera. He also composed over 360 songs, known, loved and sung whenever family groups or friends gather.

The Podhale area around Zakopane and the Tatra mountains are home to *Górale* music, or highland folk music, usually played by one lead violin or *prym*, second violins, and a three-stringed *basy*, or cello. The Brigand dance, a circle of men with clashing axes, hearkens back to the days of brigandage and derring-do. **Klezmer** music, widely played in the USA, has strong Jewish undertones. You will see the occasional didgeridoo busker in Kraków playing the Aboriginal Australian longpipe of hollowed wood.

Literature

Kraków's literary greats include poet **Adam Zagajewski**, novelist and playwright **Sławomir Mrożek** and the 1996 Nobel prize winner **Wisława Szymborska**.

With the advent of Christianity came literature. **Jan Długosz**'s (1415–80) twelve-volume *History of Poland* in Latin is great if you can remember your *amo* and *amat*. The oldest Polish text is the 13th-century former national anthem *Bogurodzica* ('Mother of God'). The 18th and 19th centuries, when Poland had been brutally partitioned, saw a slew of excellent romantic poets, much loved by homesick Poles. In 1905 **Henryk Sienkiewicz** (1846–1916) was awarded the Nobel prize for *Quo Vadis*. It was later to be one of the first cinemascope movie epics. **Władysław Reymont** won the Nobel prize for literature. **Joseph Conrad** (*Heart of Darkness*, *Typhoon*, *Lord Jim*), born

---

FRÉDÉRIC CHOPIN (1810–49)

Chopin's heart lies in an urn in the Holy Cross Church (Kościół Św. Krzyża) in Warsaw. The great composer's last residence before going into exile in France was the Czapski Palace near the home of Warsaw's Academy of Fine Arts. He would have been told of the defeat of Napoleon and would probably have approved of the 1848 revolutions in Europe. His birth name was Fryderyk Szopen. Chopin basically invented the Polish classical musical style, inspired by such poetic folk and court rythms as the *polonez* (polonaise), the *mazur* (mazurka, of which he composed 62), the *kujawiak* and the *oberek*. He started writing music at seven. He composed 26 preludes, of which 24 were written in one winter cooped up with lover and writer Ms George Sand. He died of TB at the age of 39.

Left: *Lost in the passion of her music, a street violinist attracts an enthusiastic crowd.*

Józef Konrad Korzeniowski and writing in English between 1857 and 1924, is particularly well known. **Stanisław Ignacy Witkiewicz** (Witkacy, 1885–1939) stunned society with his eclectic Bohemian writing. He is credited with creating the so-called 'Theatre of the Absurd.' **Czesław Miłosz** won the Nobel prize in 1980 for his poetry and prose.

Above: *Polish dumplings, or* pierogi, *are every budget diner's favourite.*
Opposite: *A Polish glass of beer, unlike in an English pub, is never filled to the brim.*

FOOD WORDS

Bread: *Chleb*
Fish: *Ryba*
Sugar: *Cukier*
Steak: *Befsztyk*
Milk: *Mleko*
Rice: *Ryż*
Tea: *Herbata*
Potato: *Ziemniak*
Egg: *Jajko*
Salad: *Surówka*
Chips: *Frytki*
Chicken: *Kurczak*
Fruit drink: *Napój*
Beer: *Piwo*
Menu extras in Polish English are known as Additives!

What to Eat

World cuisine, they say, peaks with the Chinese, then the Indians and then, at a pinch, the French. Poland doesn't really feature at these lofty heights, no matter the hyperbole. Sausage, cabbage, pork dumplings and potatoes are not exactly *haute cuisine*, but then a working man would probably starve on Provençal pickings.

But one does feast in Poland: helpings are huge, the dishes a blend of Russian, Jewish, German, Ukrainian, Hungarian, Lithuanian and Belarusian. Hunks of beef and pork are popular and game is common. *Pierogi* – ravioli-like dumplings filled with either minced meat or white cheese – is an inexpensive favourite (under US$5 for a meal). Order it with *barszcz* which can be a beetroot soup or, with spicy herbs, a delicious hot drink. *Zurek* is another tasty soup. *Bigos*, made with sauerkraut and chopped-up meats, takes several days and reheating to mature. But it's a home dish rather than a restaurant one.

Pubs often do not serve food. But they will always rustle up a 'toast' for you: toasted cheese with pickles. And everyone likes herring roll-mops, or a 'bekon' steak at a fast-food stall.

Near the coast or lakes, the fish dishes (*ryba*) are divine. Try *danie z trzech ryb* – steamed salmon, trout and pike. In spite of millions of Poles migrating to the USA and

Britain, the full hot English breakfast is alien to Poland, where breakfast is inevitably coffee, juice, cold meats, cheeses and bread. The more expensive the hotel, the greater the variety. You might, however, be lucky and get scrambled egg. The favourite fast food is *zapiekanki*, a sliced baguette with melted cheese served rather awkwardly on a strip of white cardboard.

Pastries from *cukiernia* shops are very good. Ice cream is Poland's great addiction – it is served in small scoops to allow you to try various flavours. A delicious one is iced nougat with blackberry sauce.

What to Drink

A mug of spiced beetroot juice, or *barszcz*, should not be missed. Poles tend to drink tea (without milk) in a glass with a dunked lemon slice. Ask for English tea and you may get a glass of milk – if your sign language falters – rather than a jug of it.

When it comes to alcohol, Poles are not as bad as Russians but they like their drink. Beers are becoming increasingly popular. They are usually draft pilsner and are not as piquant as the Czech original. There are two or three big brewery chains, all of whom have lost focus somewhere down the line. You would do better to stick to German *weissbier*.

Wines are ferociously expensive in Poland. Vodka is served chilled in shot glasses and downed in one go. There are dozens of vodkas: smarter pubs will offer you Finlandia; Zubrówka, infused with a stem of Bison grass from the forests of Białowieża in the east, has a cachet all of its own. Not to be outdone is Tatrzańska, flavoured with mountain herbs. Pieprzówki, true to its name, has a touch of pepper in it. One Polish way of drinking vodka is to lower a shot glass of vodka into your beer. *Na Zdrowie!*

VODKA

Vodka originated in Russia, but it is also made in Poland, Finland and even France. The word goes back to the Greek *hudór*, the Sanskrit *udan* ('water') and the Russian diminutive *voda*, also meaning 'water'. And tough guys drink it like water; a bottle between two is not uncommon in Poland. It is traditionally served chilled and neat in a one-shot tumbler, although the western habit of mixing it with fruit juice has crept in. Vodka is normally a clear (and mind-imploding) spirit made from grain or potatoes. But there are boutique additives: bison grass, juniper berries, honey, mountain herbs or anything that strikes your alchemic fancy. In Poland you get brownie points if you ask for local vodka, not the imported variety.

2
Kraków

Poland's second city has become first choice for most travellers to the country. In Kraków, every turn you make as you stroll along reveals an old church spire, a medieval market, or an ancient building resonant with hundreds of years of turbulent history.

WAWEL

A pretty girl sits on the low wall of the long ramp that leads up the huge walls of **Wawel Hill and Castle**. She has an easel in front of her, painting the giant breastwork and entrance gate. From every angle this vast Gothic, Renaissance and Baroque castle-cum-village on the hill is worthy of a watercolour.

Wawel overlooks a lazy loop of the wide **Vistula River** and was first occupied 2000 years ago by Vistulan (Wiślanie) hunter-gatherers and embryonic farmers who traded with the Romans. The Vistula in fact used to surround the hill until one tributary was filled in. Up over the eastern entrance gate, past the solid red brick walls, you will see a skyline of turrets, towers and cupolas, a foretaste of pleasures to come. Look down, and through the hillside trees you'll see a series of dreaming church spires – the **Bernadine church and monastery** with its multi-alcoved white statues.

Wawel is Kraków's largest and most picturesque fairy-tale conglomerate of ancient structures, visited by all who come to the city. Only first-year university students stay away, apparently – for some superstitious reason lost in the mists of academia.

DON'T MISS

*** **Wawel:** ancient hilltop castle of kings.
*** **Old Town Market Square:** vast and bustling.
*** **Old Kazimierz:** Jewish history – old synagogues and cobbled streets.
** **St Mary's Church:** Gothic star-spangled interior.
** **Auschwitz-Birkenau:** Nazi World War II death camp.
** **Floriańska and Barbakan:** huge medieval ramparts guarding the city.

Opposite: *The multi-towered Royal Cathedral on Wawel Hill.*

CHAPEL IN THE CORNER

St Adalbert was a missionary
from Prague who in AD993
began converting the tribes of
Hungary. One of the oldest
buildings in Kraków is named
after him, the rather humble
St Adalbert's Church tucked
away in one corner of Market
Square. In front of it you may
see a drama student in G.I. Joe
uniform, leaning on his rifle,
absolutely motionless. Some
say Adalbert actually preached
here. He died a martyr as
many missionaries did at these
times of fierce pagan-Christian
conflict. The little square
church with its double-storey
green Baroque cupola was initially part of Wawel Castle's
extended defences. The first
Romanesque church built
there goes back 1000 years,
with possibly a wooden one
before that.

Crusader Towers ★★★

You pass the Senator's, Teczyńska, Noble and Maiden
towers and finally the rounded red-capped Sandomierz
Tower, all great chess-like castles in themselves, soaring
upwards in brute vigilance, defying all attackers. On your
left is the city; far below, the swans, pleasure boats and
picnic lawns along the Vistula.

If you have missed breakfast, pop into the **Restauracja
Na Wawelu** beneath the trees for a milkshake, iced nougat
or pot of tea served in glistening china. It faces onto the
ivy-covered back of the old **Castle Hospital**.

Dragon's Lair ★★

You now have a choice. Turn west to the **Dragon's Cave**
on the edge of the hill, where the brave shoemaker's
apprentice, Kuba Dratewka, won the heart of the king's
daughter by tricking and killing a dragon, or go into the
main grassy courtyard of the **castle** itself. There's time for
both. Smok Wawelski, the magic dragon, lived in a cave
beneath the 1300-year-old castle of Krak. Its a full 135
spiral steps down into the cave (called **Smocza Jama**),
expecting with every step to come face to face with a
jagged fire-breathing monster. The interior of the cave is
70m (230ft) across. It emerges into the sunlight right next
to a fire-roaring dragon, the work of sculptor **Bronisław
Chromy**. There are few shaking Kraków children that have
not had their photo taken next to him.

On the horizon, beyond the Vistula, you'll be able
to see the great grass-covered man-made **Kościuszko**
mound-pyramid.

Castle Grounds ★★★

As you leave the Thieves Tower and walk into the main
grounds of the castle, with its trees and greenery, turn right
for a magnificent panorama of the multidomed and multi-
turreted **Wawel Cathedral**, the country's pride and joy.

The ticket office choice for the castle includes State
Rooms, Royal Apartments, Crown Treasury and Armoury,
Oriental Art, the 'Lost Wawel', and the Royal Garden
Tour. All are separately priced and none cheap.

Temporary exhibitions (near the ticket office) could include sculptor **Lucjan Myrta**'s 40 years of working in *bursztyn* or amber. His masterpiece is a jewel cabinet. It weighs 955kg (2100lb) and stands taller than a man. Not since the days of the 17th-century Gdańsk amber workshops has there been such an incredibly detailed and glittering piece of work. It hits

Above: *Wawel Royal Castle is now a multi-chamber museum.*

you like the tomb of a long-lost pharaoh. Also on view are vases, lamps, candle holders and clocks, plus – from the artist's 13,000-piece collection – a fossilized lizard and tick trapped in amber millions of years ago.

The ticket office also houses the information office, restaurant, toilets and post office. Guided tours can be booked and there is a shop selling Polish folk music. The outdoor café beneath the trees further on is a popular spot for artists to paint the lovely matching integrity of the cathedral's many domes and towers. The gardens cover about 2.5ha (6 acres).

Forever Lost

The grassy courtyard of Wawel Castle looks as if you've wandered into some ancient Roman ruins. In fact this area (please do not walk on the grass) up until 200 years ago was full of houses, possibly even supply shops, stables, coachhouses and was, of course, a hub of activity. These almost grassed-over foundation stones were once two 12th-century medieval churches and a vicarage belonging to one Canon Jan Borek. They were destroyed by the invading Austrians in 1803–04 and replaced by a drill ground for their troops. There is a **Lost Wawel Exhibition** in the basement of what was once the **Royal Kitchens** with virtual reality computer technology enabling visitors to travel back to the 10th century and see what Wawel

---

PUFFED-UP DRAGON

Once upon a time, living in a cave beneath Wawel Hill there was a fire-breathing dragon (Smok Wawelski) who gobbled up sheep, cattle and occasionally young maidens. King Krak offered the hand of his beautiful daughter Wanda to any man who would slay the beast. A young apprentice shoemaker, Kuba, accepted the challenge and tricked the dragon into eating a sheep skin stuffed with tar and sulphur. The heat in its stomach was too much. It jumped into the Vistula, to drink until it burst. And all, bar the dragon, lived happily ever after.

There are 135 steps leading down to the Dragon's Lair, or *Smocza Jama*, at Wawel Hill and 145m (476ft) of tunnels.

CURSE OF THE TOMB

Ancient tombs can be deadly.
Not because they have
Transylvanian vampires, spring
daggers or pyramid cobra-
guards, but because they
contain the *Aspergillus flavus*
fungus, which causes a rare
fungal infection of the mucous
membranes and lungs. The
fate of the archaeologists who
discovered the 3500-year-old
tomb of Tutankhamun in 1922
was similar to that of Polish
archeologists who exhumed
and examined the remains of
Kazimierz Jagiellończyk (son
of King Władysław Jagieło) in
the 1970s. Within 10 years,
15 of those involved had died,
one within six months.

looked like in those ancient days when it was the
'Rotunda' of the Virgin Mary, the seat or palladium of
Wawel's first ruler. There were up to ten churches on
Wawel Hill at one time.

Wawel Cathedral ★★★

The entrance to the cathedral is tiny considering the size of
this massive basilica, the third cathedral to be built in
Wawel. The first was built in AD1000, followed by a late
11th-century church that burned down 100 years later and
then this 'modern' one built in 1320–64. Incidentally, it's
quite useful to employ a guide to really appreciate the
church's treasures. Check with the good nun selling tickets.

Up the entrance stairway and chained to the wall there
are, for some extraordinary reason, the forlorn skulls of a
rhino, a whale and what looks like an elephant. They do
nothing for anyone other than encourage the legend that
should they fall, the world will come to an end.

The cathedral embodies the 1000-year history and
pride of Kraków. It was built by Władysław (the Short) to
entomb the relics of **St Stanisław** who came to a sticky
end in his political Church versus State scrap with King
Bolesław (the Generous) in 1079. You can easily spend a
morning inside the cathedral. It is a repository for some
important Polish art and treasure. As **Pope John Paul II** put
it when he was bishop of the city: 'The Sanctuary of the
nation cannot be entered without inner trembling, and
awe, for here is contained a vast greatness which cries out
to us of Poland's history, of all our pasts.'

The Crypts ★★

There are crypts housing the massive tombs and remains
of 41 kings of Poland, as well as other distinguished citizens. Towards the centre of the church is the **Poets' Crypt**.
Juliusz Słowacki and Adam Mickiewicz (1798–1855 – his
Pan Tadeusz is Poland's national epic) are both buried
here. It was customary to have coffins and bodies interred
under the floor of a church in a fabulous sarcophagus and
sometimes with a chapel built on top. But then everyone
ran out of floor space so **Zygmund (the Old)** decided on a

crypt under his Zygmund Chapel. This latter has a double-layered monument, one for him and one for his son Zygmund August.

The AD1100 **St Leonard's Crypt** is a wonder. With its chunky columns and cross vaults it is the only surviving Romanesque area of the cathedral. Huge great stones make up its sombre Baroque – free walls and a small altar at one end. Zygmund's coffin is made of stone but the rest are chiselled highly decorated metal.

Above: The Renaissance balustraded courtyard of Wawel Castle seems to float in the air.

Sigismund Chapel ★★★

The gilded as opposed to copper-domed cupola flashes in the sun on top of this square royal chapel. It is regularly restored and polished. The chapel was designed for King Zygmund (or Sigismund) the Old by Florentine architect **Bartolomeo Berricci** and is a masterpiece of the Polish Renaissance. It took nine years to complete and was finished in 1533, with lavish gilding and a clever blending of marble and sandstone carvings. The altarpiece was created from a design by Germany's great artist, **Albrecht Dürer**. The walls are covered with sculpted decorations.

A Tomb or Two ★★

Apart from the father and son tombs of the Zygmunds, there are many other marvellously carved tombs, ranging from the high, sculpted sarcophagus of **King Kazimierz** designed by Veit Stoss in 1492 to the 1760 tomb behind the high altar of **King Jan III Sobieski** (all Baroque cherubs), while the tomb of **King Stefan Batory** was cut in 1595 by sculptor Santi Gucci. The **Canopy of St Stanisław** on the cathedral's largest altar is made of silver, the coffin supported by angels.

> #### FOR WHOM THE BELL TOLLS
>
> Touch the heart or 'clapper' of the Zygmund Bell in the Royal Cathedral on Wawel Hill and your dreams of love may materialize, especially if you touch it with your left hand, the one nearest to your heart.
>
> This legend dates back to 1520 when a young girl's dream of marriage actually came true. So they say.
>
> The bell weighs 11 tonnes, and has a diameter of 2.5m (8ft). The clapper is rarely used except during significant church ceremonies or events.

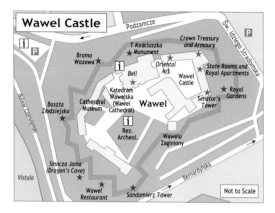

Wawel Castle

Podzamcze

T Kościuszka Monument

Crown Treasury and Armoury

Św. Idziego Stradomska

Brama Wazowa

Bell

Oriental Art

State Rooms and Royal Apartments

Wawel Castle

Baszta Złodziejska

Katedram Wawelska (Wawel Cathedral)

Catherdral Museum

Wawel

Senator's Tower

Royal Gardens

Rez. Archeol.

Wawelu Zaginiony

Bulwar Czerwieński

Smocza Jama (Dragon's Cave)

Vistula

Bernardyńska

Wawel Restaurant

Sandomierz Tower

Not to Scale

The Castle ★★★

Kazimierz (the Restorer) started the castle off with Romanesque, then Władysław (the Short) and finally Kazimierz (the Great) all had a Gothic go at it, building according to the taste and style of their time. But it was left to Zygmunt (the Old) to convert it into a Renaissance Italian palazzo in the early 1500s. As soon as you go through the echoing entrance arch – 'If God is with us, who is against us?' it reads in Latin – into the courtyard you are struck by the numerous delicate purple columns and Bartolomeo Berricci's rounded Venetian arches, each the height of four men, row on row, reaching up to the carefully snow-sloped red roof: a huge square three-storey fairy-arcaded castle, flanked by towers at each corner. And there is nothing small about it: there are 71 rooms and some 700m² (75,000 sq ft) of interior space.

Touring the Castle

There are four separate tours. The first is **Oriental Art in the West Wing**. It is not very Oriental, more Middle Eastern, mainly the collection of King Sobieski's loot from the defeat of the Turks at Vienna in 1683. The embroidered Turkish tents, armour, silk banners and Persian rugs are exotic, particularly the stunning sabre of Grand Vizier Kara Mustafa.

The **Crown Treasury and Armoury** does not have much in the way of exotic jewellery. Kraków has had too many invaders for that. The Prussians, for example, took the coronation insignia in 1795, melting down the crown. There is the 13th-century jagged sword, or Szczerbiec, used at coronations, the crown of Zygmunt I, a 1533 royal banner and King Kazimierz's 14th-century goblet. The oldest piece used to be a 10th-century rock crystal pendant, but in fact a 5th-century ring with a Latin inscription now takes honours.

A halberd is a killing combo of axe, pick and spear on one shaft – a favourite, for example, in the English civil war of the 17th century – and there are plenty of these in the Armoury. There are also rapiers, Spanish daggers, suits of armour (including armadillo-like scale armour), cannons, guns, crossbows and just about every type of close-quarter killing machine known to man. They date mainly from the 15–17th centuries. There are copies of banners flown during the famous Battle of Grunwald which saw the end of the Teutonic Knights.

The **State Rooms and Royal Apartments** are sumptuous: furniture, dozens of tapestries, paintings, *objets d'art*, let alone the incredible box-like ceiling paintings and fretted woodwork, fit for a king indeed. No wonder there's an eagle-eyed walkie-talkie guard wherever you turn, though the size of some of the tapestries would make it tricky to pop them into your pocket. In the Audience Hall there are 30 sculptured heads on the ceiling, all made of wood. None are supermodels.

You'll be able to visit the bedroom, study, Tournament Hall (where council meetings were held), the Room of the Army, Inspection Hall, Zodiac Room and Planet Room. Then comes the hall of the 1514 Battle of Orsha, with dozens of portraits, the Bird Room (its walls are covered in red and yellow leather), Eagle Room (Royal Court of Justice), Chapel and, most incredible of all, the lush candelabra-lit, glittering and highly polished Senators' Hall with intricate tapestries almost the width of the room. The Nazis used it as a cinema.

The **Royal Apartments**, once again with ornamental gilt ceiling squares, include the Royal Dining Room, bedroom and the tiny black, white and gold 'Cock's Foot' rooms which, according to one reporter, were 'probably used by Zygmund III for resting.' The oldest tapestry – of which there are many in the castle – is in the royal bedroom: *Knight and Swan*, a languid medieval tale.

MARKET SQUARE ★★★

In size, only St Mark's Square in Venice competes with Kraków's Main Market Square, or **Rynek Główny**, as the

---

CHAPELS

The word 'chapel' comes from the Latin word *capella*, meaning a small cloak or cap, from where the cloak of St Martin of Tours was originally kept 1600 years ago in France. There are 20 such chapels in Wawel Cathedral, including:

Trinity Chapel – 1431.

Czartoryski Chapel – underneath the clock tower; access to royal tombs.

Lipski Chapel – 14th century; Gothic; dome paintings.

Bishop Gamrat Chapel – behind the main altar; silver coffin containing 800-year-old relics.

King Jan Olbracht Chapel – the sarcophagus of Kazimierz the Great faces this chapel.

Chapel of Bishop Zadzik – originally a royal coronation dressing room.

Sigismund Chapel – nearby is the sarcophagus of Queen Jadwiga (1374–99); white Carrara marble.

largest medieval square in Europe. Visualize an enormous empty space 200m (219yd) wide by 200m long as big as a football field, surrounded by 11 massive blocks of ancient buildings and palaces, in themselves separated by 12 narrow streets. Right in the middle is the long (100m/ 109yd) treble-storey arcaded old **Cloth Hall and Tower**. At one corner is the majestic twin-towered **St Mary's Church**, a Gothic red brick basilica that goes back to 1355, some 650 years.

Now, imagine what the square was like when first built. Think of a Breughel painting. It was the centre of town, the hub of every activity: horses, carts, crowds of jostling people, chickens for sale, pigs on rope leads, wool cloth from England, delicacies from Russia. The smell of horse manure would have been everywhere in the mud and dust and slush. Perhaps there would be the whisper of a public execution that day, or a coronation next week. Church bells would ring out. There'd be the noise of a thousand shouting, laughing, haggling voices. Entertainment-wise, the square would have been the equivalent of a pop festival, TV and football match combined, with jugglers, knife-sharpeners, beer sellers, violin players, pickpockets, seducers, armed men in leather jerkins and pointy shoes, and ladies in long embroidered pinafores.

In many ways it has not changed. The Cloth Hall stalls sell amber jewellery (they can also fix a broken bracelet), the trumpet calls from St Mary's tower, a statue artist dressed as a bushy tree poses, pigeons fight for crumbs in seed pens, hackney cabs in proud brass clip-clop past, flower ladies arrange their wares, a trio in traditional costume plays Zakopane music, ladies in head scarves go off to pray. There are cafés, a bag lady checking out a rubbish bin, exotic ice-cream sundaes served under awnings, junk souvenirs, fast-food snacks. There's a building-sized advert of Pierce Brosnan; a wailing police car inches its way through the crowd; a man with half-filled glasses at his collapsible table plays a Peruvian flute tune watched by children. And everywhere you see the flash of digital cameras. 'We are from Honduras, please you take photo.'

Opposite: *Kraków's Market Square was the largest in medieval Europe. The Cloth Hall is on the right and St Mary's Church at the centre.*

North Side of the Square

Kraków was planned in 1257. There used to be many buildings, some quick built, in the square. Only the **Town Hall Tower** and **Cloth Hall** have survived the centuries. The north side has a lot of restaurants, flower sellers and the hackney cab rank. The three northern blocks include the **Deer House**, where Tsar Nicholas I and Goethe both stayed when it was a public inn; **Eagle House** (Dom Pod Orłem) features a raptor sculpture with a snake in its talons, and the **Margrave's House** (a Margrave ranked above a count in German nobility) has a fancy golden Rococo portal.

The South Side

In one corner, nearest the Grodzka exit street, is the **Duke's House** (No. 26) where 500 years ago the magical sorcerer Master Twardowski was supposed to have weaved his spells. Today, perhaps in spiritual revenge, the house is adorned with a rather melancholy-looking statue of the Italian Saint Giovanni da Capistrano, patron saint of judges and a peripatetic preacher who came to Kraków in 1450 to deliver sermons in the Market Square. **Wierznek House** (No. 16), at the other end of the block, is named after Mikołaj Wierznek who in 1363 at the Congress of Kraków put on a lavish feast for King Kazimierz of Poland and the kings of Rome, Bohemia, Hungary, Cyprus and Denmark. Having no choice, Kazimierz's daughter was married off to the king of Germany-Bohemia. The restaurant is still called Wierznek.

The East Side

The **Grey House** at No. 6 is known as **Kamienica Szara**. Kazimierz the Great's lady love, Sara, lived here and the Szara restaurant with its seated

FAMILY FEUD

The two towers of St Mary's in Kraków are totally different. Legend has it that two brothers built the towers. When the elder brother realized his tower was going to be shorter (he hadn't done sufficient preparation), he killed the younger in a fit of jealousy, and then threw himself off his own tower. The dreadful murder weapon, an iron knife, is supposedly the one hanging in the Cloth Hall or Sukiennice in Market Square. But alas, the truth is that that knife only served to remind the townsfolk to be good. And both towers were originally the same height, extra storeys on the one having been added later – which goes to show how historians can ruin a good story.

Below: *Market Square has dozens of restaurants. But the drinks can be expensive.*

chef sign is still popular. Next door is the **Italian House**, once owned by wealthy Italian bankers. The high arch allowed coaches to pass under it to Poland's first post office. Two medieval fighting lizards decorate one window arch on **Kamienica pod Jaszczurami**, possibly designed by a pupil of Veit Stoss, the talented carver of the wooden altar in St Mary's Church. At No. 9 is **Boner House** whose parapet stands out from the rest on this side of the square, because it is higher and more intricately designed. Originally Gothic, it is now Renaissance in style, with curves, loops and towerettes.

The West Side

The famous Piwnica pod Baranami grand cabaret in the huge **Palace of the Rams** has been drawing crowds of poets, artists and music-lovers for half a century. Its name comes from the days when there was an inn here, its supply of meat and sheep kept in adjacent pens, some 700 years ago. Rams' heads decorate the corners. The fare the cabaret put on was not Lloyd Webber; it was much more politically and socially critical, and often, during Communist times, dangerously irritating to the authorities. It was the cabaret tradition of Liza Minnelli, Jacques Brel and Paris' *Chat Noir*. Piotr Skrzynecki was the leading light. **Pod Krzysztofory Palace** (No. 35) is a composite of three Gothic townhouses, now owned by the Wodzicki family. The palace is home to the fascinating **Museum of Kraków**. Next door is the **Spiski Palace** and its elegant arcaded-entrance **Hawelka Restaurant**, for diners with deep pockets.

Cloth Hall ★★★

The 108m (354ft) **Cloth Hall**, or **Sukiennice**, dominates the middle of Market Square. In fact it looks like a palace, with Baroque

towers and Renaissance parapets, the whole flanked by
18 neo-Gothic arches and classical pillars in tiers on
either side. It started life as two rather run-down rows of
stalls selling German and Flemish cloth. A roof was
added, then came a ring of butchers' shops. In 1555 it
was all but destroyed by fire. Rebuilt, it now included a
very elegant attic, much copied as the 'Polish' attic.
Restoration in the late 19th century included the addition
of rows of coats of arms inside. In 1883 Polish paintings
were displayed in the Cloth Hall for the first time. Today,
in four major rooms, the **Gallery** exhibits some 1500
paintings including the outstanding 'Peasants and Jews'
masterpieces of Piotr Michałowski. The hall itself no
longer sells the woollen cloth of yesteryear but trades
briskly in amber, jewellery, crafts and curios in the tiny
one-person stalls. If you get shopping fatigue, pop into the
Noworolski Café with its Art Nouveau ambience for a
leisurely coffee.

THE MUSEUMS OF KRAKÓW

There are at least 25 museums in Kraków, ranging from
the **National Museum of Art** (al. 3 Majal) to the **Pharmacy
Museum** (ul. Floriańska 25). The **City Engineering
Museum** (ul. Św. Wawrzyńca 15) is sited inside an old
tram depot and features modes of transport over the years
together with a hands-on 'Fun and Science' exhibition for
young folk. The **Ethnographical Museum** (pl. Wolnica 1)
will take you back to Poland's early peasant folk days. It
even has wooden bicycles and some lovely Kraków
Christmas cribs. It is well worth a visit, as is the **History
Museum** (Rynek Główny 35), tracing Kraków's past from
1257. There is a **History of Photography Museum**, the
Manggha Japanese Arts Museum, **Home Army Museum**
(concentrating on World War II Resistance), and the Art
Nouveau works of Wyspiański in the museum of the same
name. The **National Museum** has recently opened a new
Gallery of 20th-century Polish Art.

Admission to the museums varies but is in the region
of 7zł. You can count on 10:00 as an average opening
time, closing 16:00–18:00.

CHRISTMAS CRIBS

In South Island, New Zealand,
a crib is a weekend holiday
cottage. But in Kraków, a crib
or *szopka* is a beautifully
decorated handmade
Christmas crib. Giovanni di
Bernadone, better known as
Francis of Assisi, started the
practice. The Jesuits took it to
Austria and the Franciscans to
Poland. Miniatures have been
crafted in Kraków since the
13th century and a competition for the best one is held on
the first Thursday of December
at the foot of the statue of
Adam Mickiewicz – the
patriotic writer – in Market
Square. Made of wood, silver
foil, fairy lights and cardboard,
the Kraków *szopki* always
have Kraków castles, palaces
and churches (particularly St
Mary's Gothic Cathedral) as
backdrops. Sometimes they
even feature local celebrities.

Above: *The star-spangled ceiling of St Mary's Church in Kraków is typically Gothic.*

Collegium Maius ★★

The arcaded Gothic cloister courtyard of Collegium Maius goes back to 1400 when a corner house was purchased by the king for the **Kraków Academy**, the oldest university building in Poland. It is not dissimilar to an old Oxford College. The Collegium Maius is the seat of the **Jagiellonian University Museum**, whose collections include historic scientific instruments for cartography, meteorology, astronomy, physics and chemistry. The most venerable of these is the delicate 1054 Arabian astrolabe, a sort of early sextant used in star navigation. The words *America noviter reperta* are printed on what is known as the 1510 **Jagiellonian Globe**, the first mention in the world of the American continent. There is a permanent **Exhibition of Medieval Art**. The museum is open mornings only (ul. Jagiellońska 15, tel: 4812 422 0549, e-mail: info@maius.in.uj.edu.pl).

Barbakan ★★

A 'barbican' in English is a watchtower or fortified out-work projecting from a medieval rampart to protect a drawbridge or entrance gate. The one in Kraków is massive. Red-brick, round and hugely Gothic (1499), it is every photographer's favourite subject. It guards the entrance to the **Floriańska Gate** – the main gate, past huge bastion walls – into the old medieval city. The Barbakan outside the Floriańska is a busy spot, with colourfully dressed Polish folk singers (and even an occasional Native American group), crowds of visitors, bagel vendors and the rattle of trams along circular Basztowa Street.

The Barbakan looks like a Disneyland version of a fairytale castle complete with seven witch-capped towers. The Floriańska Gate goes back to the 13th century. Its interior ramparts on one side are covered with bright if dubious works of art for sale and further afield are a plethora of churches. It leads into Kraków's busiest approach street to the old Market Square, ulica Floriańska.

Floriańska Street is a popular, narrow pedestrian street with busy boutiques, money-changers and restaurants. But if you explore it you'll come across such historical gems as **Pod Róża** (No. 14), the oldest hotel in Kraków.

CATHOLIC KRAKÓW

Once the indefatigable Saint Paul had taken Christianity to Rome, and 200 years later Emperor Constantine converted, Christianity soon became entwined in the Empire's hierarchical system, with a

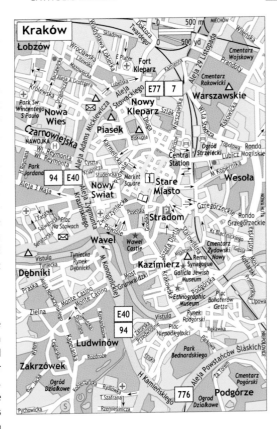

Caesar, Tsar or Pope at the top of a huge bureaucratic pyramid. Conversion was often not a question of individual piety or mystical discovery but rather it became an astute political juggling by rulers to acquire land, or to protect themselves from others already converted from 'paganism'.

Thus it was in Poland. In 965 **Mieszko I** underwent public baptism, so carefully placing himself under the protection of Europe's most influential axis of power, the **Papacy**. Naturally his fellow Polonians did likewise. Poland was now Catholic and, with a few Protestant hiccups, has been ever since.

BUGLES IN THE BELFRY

The practice of sounding a bugle alarm is common to several Polish cities, but particularly St Mary's in Kraków. The *hejnal* bugle call was originally blasted out twice a day but from the 16th century, a time of great danger, it was blown on the hour every hour. It is sounded – to the cheers of visitors looking up – to all four corners of Kraków's Rynek or Market Square, from the highest of the two church towers. It only has five notes and it stops mid-bar. The poet Bulat Okudzhava in his *Farewell to Poland* writes: 'When the *hejnal* calls to the sky, my horse pricks up its ears and my hand reaches for my sword.' Poles relish a little goose-pimple patriotism.

St Mary's Church ★★★

Founded in 1226, destroyed by Tatars in 1241 and replaced in about 1290 by today's church, St Mary's is part Romanesque and part Gothic. Facing the Market Square, it has two entirely different **towers**. The taller, at 81m (266ft), looks like a fairy queen's headpiece out of Camelot. The other, more sober, has five bells.

St Mary's Church is mainly Gothic but many additions were created down the centuries, particularly the side chapels. The cathedral, with its wealth of detail on the outside, can best be studied through binoculars: there are floral motifs, exquisite arches and sculpted figures, each telling a biblical story. It's as if the masons really were working for the glory of God, knowing that few humans would ever see their work.

The presbytery is also topped with 21 sculptured columns. **Plac Mariacki** faces the main visitor entrance which has iron fetters, or *kuna*, to the side of it. The main front entrance is reserved for actual worshippers. The Plac features a fountain statue of a pensive student, much loved by teachers and their busy school groups.

Wooden Masterpiece

It cost as much as an average town's annual budget – 2808 florins – and 12 years (1477–89) for German sculptor **Veit Stoss** (Wit Stwosz in Polish) to carve the **high altar** backdrop inside St Mary's. It is completely made of wood and features 200 figures and 2000 details. Brown, midnight blue, gold, it is a truly magnificent work of art. The material used for Poland's masterpiece was mainly 500-year-old limewood trees, although the boarding is made of larch. The statues are all gilded and painted – not unlike some delicate Chinese ivory on a massive scale. There are **twelve panels**, known as a pentaptych, with a centrepiece and double wing. The width is 11m (36ft) and the height 12.8m (42ft). The tallest figures are 2.8m (9ft), the smallest 3cm (1 in). Pablo Picasso called it the eighth wonder of the world. The arched stone above is vaulted in spangled stars and gilt with brightly coloured wall decorations or friezes by **Jan Matejko**, the doyen of Polish 19th-century artists.

Opposite: *Statues of the Twelve Apostles line the entrance façade of the 1596 Baroque Church of Sts Peter and Paul.*

Veit Stoss also made the huge stone **crucifix** in the central nave. The whole interior is a wonderland of rainbow colour especially when fully lit. The **stained-glass windows** behind the high altar rise in three slender arches, each with 40 twinkling multicoloured panels. When the sun is behind them they are magic. Each brick in the Middle Ages was hand-crafted, creating fabulous patterns by using different colours of binder and deliberately unevenly fired bricks – anything from the usual red-brown to dark black, with some glazed to a green colour.

Dominican Church ★★

Its feathered, flame-tipped red-brick exterior reaches up like an Aztec headdress. Sited at 12 ul. Stolarska, south of the Main Square, this, the 13th-century St Trinity Church, was badly damaged in the Tatar raid of 1241 and again by fire in 1850, then restored. It has a variety of interesting side chapels. **St Jacek's Chapel** is reached by stone steps on the left as you enter. He was the first prior and died in 1257. **St Hyacinth's Chapel** and its sequence of paintings is another. The **Rosary Chapel** was built to commemorate Jan Sobieski's victory over the Turks in 1683 at Vienna. Defeated Grand Vizier Kara Mustafa, as custom dictated, had one of his men strangle him with a silken cord.

Franciscan Church ★★★

It was in this church in 1385 that the 'pagan' Grand Duke Jogaila of Lithuania was baptized and became **Władysław Jagieło**, king of Poland. Strangely for a medieval church, founded in 1237, its interior is decorated with Art Nouveau **stained-glass windows**. Designed by **Stanisław Wyspiański**, they are incredibly striking in their panoply of blues and

THE BLACK MADONNA

In thousands of Polish churches you will find a copy of the 600-year-old Mary and Child Jesus icon, the original of which is in the hilltop Jasna Góra monastery in the town of Częstochowa 140km (87 miles) northwest of Kraków. For Polish Catholics, a chance to see the Black Madonna is a lifetime experience almost akin to Islam's Hajj. It is Poland's holiest shrine and was never captured by any of Poland's many enemies. Of unknown origin, it was probably painted between 500 and 1300 years ago on a wooden panel 122 x 82cm (49 x 33in, or roughly 4 x 3ft). The Black Madonna is revered by enraptured, tearful pilgrims as the 'Queen of Poland', spiritual and political resistance symbol down the ages. Tradition has it that it was painted by St Luke. It is 'Black' because of its intense shading, its age and hundreds of years of exposure to incense.

KRAKÓW'S SEASONS

Winter: Christmas Fair, Market Square. Christmas decorations, jewellery and Galician mulled wine. New Year's Concert in Kraków's Philharmonic Hall. *Szopki* (crib-making) contest in Market Square.
Spring: Kraków Film Festival (May), Europe's oldest. Emaus at the Norbetine nunnery in Zwierzniec, near Zamość, on Easter Monday. Stalls and dousing ladies with water pistols.
Summer: Festival of Jewish Culture, Music and Dance, a Lajkonik frolic. First Thursday after Corpus Christi feast day. If the fancy-dressed Tatar on a wooden hobby horse touches you with his wand, you'll be lovestruck.
Autumn: Market Square parade of dogs. Largest dachshund gets the prize. Rotunda Culture Centre: Festival of Celtic poetry dance and Music, the Magic Green Island Folk Festival.

yellows, especially the 'God the Father – Become' panel above the main doors. It is large: 8.5m x 3.90m (28ft x 13ft). Every Friday during Lent (the 40 days leading up to Easter) black-hooded friars hold their well-attended 400-year-old Brotherhood of God death procession to the **high altar**. The 15th-century **cloisters** have superb Gothic, Renaissance and Baroque murals.

Church of Sts Peter and Paul ★★

The intellectual Dominicans, the gentle Franciscans, and now the 'hard guys' of the Vatican and the Catholic Counter-Reformation: the **Jesuits**. The **Society of Jesus** was founded by Spanish soldier Ignacius Loyola in 1534. Their white-façaded church, its entrance lined with huge statues of the 12 apostles à la St Peter's in Rome, was the first Baroque church in Kraków, but it is permeated with the lively spirit of the Renaissance. The church is built in the form of a Latin cross, topped with a large ochre dome. The bronze **baptismal font** near one of the pillars supporting the dome goes back to 1528.

St Andrew's Church ★★

A small square with a statue of Skarga, the much liked priest, faces both the church of Sts Peter and Paul and the completely different church of St Andrew. The latter

has identical **twin towers** of austere white stone, topped with frilly Baroque cupolas. Originally a Romanesque church built in 1079–98, it is in fact one of the oldest churches and oldest surviving buildings in the whole of Poland. The interior – like in so many churches in Europe in the 18th century – was subjected to a seriously Baroque springclean, which didn't improve it at all.

The walls, Romanesque style, are 160cm (63 in) thick and the thin slit windows were obviously meant for crossbow defence – the Tatars were successfully fought off in 1241. The 1685 **altar** is made of black marble while the gilt-adorned **pulpit** is shaped like a boat.

In the square below, you will see youngsters on skateboards and perhaps hear the lovely strains of a violinist.

Map: Kraków City Centre

Labels include: Gruwald Battle Monument, Barbakan, Central Station, Ogród Florianka, Planty Gardens, Florianska, NOWA HUTA, FRANCUSKI, Planty Gardens, Lubicz, Plac Szczepański, POD POLLERA, GRAND, RÓŻA, Plac Św Ducha, EUROPEJSKI, ELEKTOR, Planty Gardens, St Anne's Theatre, Old Town Hall Tower, History Museum, Market Square, Plac Mariacki, St Mary's, AMADEUS, Mikołajska, Kopernika, Cloth Hall, SIENNA, St Adalberts, DOM POLONII, Stare Miasto, Kościół Św Józefa, Poczta Glowna, Pomnik Jana Pawla I, Plac Wszystkich Świętych, Dominican Church, Franciscan Church, WAWEL TOURIST, Smolensk, RADISSON SAS, Poselska, Palac Pugetów, Planty Gardens, St Peter & St Peter & St Paul, Boisko Miedzyszkolne, SZS, Plac Św Marii Magdaleny, St Andrew's Church, Stradom, COPERNICUS, Podzamcze, Muzeum Przyrodnicze PAN, Vistula, Wawel Castle, Wawel Cathedral, ROYAL, Bernadine Church, Synagoga Postepowa Tempel

Scale: 0 — 125 m / 0 — 125 yd

St Anne's Church ★★

St Anne was the mother of Mary, grandmother of Jesus. The church is near the Collegium Maius on ul. Św Anny. It is another **Baroque church**, highly decorated in gold and marble with murals, twirls and cherubs, surprisingly homogenous in this instance. Built in the late 17th century by the ubiquitous **Tylman van Gameren**, it is the university church.

Church on the Rock ★★

This large church overlooks Podgórska embankment and the Vistula. It is a **Pauline church** of the Order of Saint Paul the First Hermit, founded in Hungary in 1263. Formerly a place of 'pagan' worship, this church was built in 1079 and rebuilt three times. The interior today is late 18th-century Baroque and filled with the usual columns and colour. It was also the tomb of **St Stanisław** until his body was moved to Wawel Cathedral. Stanisław, the Bishop of Kraków, was murdered by King Bolesław (the Generous) in Skałka Church in Kazimierz in 1079 with seven sword blows to the head – echoes of England's Thomas à Becket.

Opposite: *An elegant hackney cab is a great way to see Kraków's historic sights.*

Above: *A Kazimierz flea market offers 'antiques', paintings and collectibles.*

Beneath the massive church and monastery (walk down narrow Paulińska Meiselsa off Krakówska to reach the church) in a beautifully decorated oval crypt cut into the hillside rock are the 13 massive tombs of such Polish greats as **Winscerty Pol** (poet), **Stanisław Wyspiański** (dramatist), **Tadeusz Banachiewicz** (astronomer and mathematician) and Nobel prize-winning poet **Czesław Miłosz** who died in 2004, aged 93.

Skałka is one of three hills defining the geography of Kraków, the others being Salvator and Wawel.

JEWISH KRAKÓW

Kraków has always been home to a large Jewish population. Descended from the ancient Israelites, the Jews based their lives on the Talmud, the Torah and on the biblical Old Testament. They were forced to abandon Palestine, retreating under Roman attack. Like the Christians they headed west in a diaspora that took them all over Europe where they were often persecuted, or moved on, as they were perceived to be unwelcome 'immigrants', trading competitors, harbingers of the plague and 'Jesus' killers'. Expelled from one country after another, many made it to a relatively safer Poland.

Booksellers

The Jewish business centre in Kraków was originally in or near Kraków's **Market Square** or **Rynek Główny**, until they were expelled by hype, hatred and hypocrisy – particularly that of Jan Kapistrano, the papal legate – in the 13th century. It was once a densely built-up area with Renaissance granary, foundry, Gothic Town Hall, vast weighing scales and bustling market stalls. The top floor of the massive **Cloth Hall** is now the **National Museum's Gallery of Polish Art**. It includes three works by Jewish painter **Maurycy Gottlieb** who died at the age of 23. The statue of poet **Adam Mickiewicz** stands between St Mary's Church and the Cloth Hall, usually surrounded by buskers, school children and souvenir hawkers. He was always generous to the Jewish community.

The Jewish merchants traditionally occupied that section of the Market Square between St Wojciech's Church and Adam Mickiewicz's statue, and the 'Grey' tenement. Book-selling was pioneered by the Jews – being a particularly literate people – and this they did on Market Square. Door-to-door selling was forbidden.

Attack

St Anne's Church in Św Anny was where the 1407 anti-Jewish pogrom ignited. **The Jewish Gate**, part of the old medieval city wall, was not far from here in **Planty Park**. It led to the **Jewish Cemetery**, today's ul. Czysta. Nothing is left of either. The Orthodox church at 24 ul. Szpitalna was the former Ahawat Raim prayer house. Hospitals for the poor were where today's lavish **Opera House** is sited. The latter was built by **Jan Zawiejski**, descended from the Jewish Feintuch family. The Szpitalna area itself consisted mainly of Jewish antiquarian shops before World War II. There is a plaque at 38 ul. Szpitalna in memory of the attack on the **Cyganeria** or **Bohemia Café**, popular with German officers, on 22 December 1942 by the Jewish underground, the ZOB.

Below: *A stained-glass window in Tempel Synagogue featuring a menorah, or seven-branched candelabrum, an emblem of Judaism.*

King's Way

Ul. Grodska leads eventually to the **Royal Wawel Castle**. Past the Dominikański crossroad on the left, at numbers 28 and 30 ul. Grodska, there was in 1913 a **Jewish prayer house**. In the years 1879–1939 there was a **Hebrew**

printing house, Fizner, publishers of the world-famous journal *Hazman*. Where ul. Grodzka ends, there used to be a gate used by Jews in medieval times, and another called the **Goldsmiths' Gate** with access to Market Square from the main Jewish residential area of Kazimierz.

Love Story

The Polish king **Kazimierz the Great** (1333–70) was particularly decent to the Jewish immigrants coming into Poland. He fell in love with **Ester**, the daughter of a Jewish tailor from Opoczno, a small village 50km (31miles) west of Radom. He apparently had three children with her (he was already married) – two sons who stayed at court and were raised as Christians and a daughter brought up as a Jew by her mother. From here on the story becomes a touch 'penny romance'. In Kazimierz there is a street called after her, ul. Estery. On the other hand, 46 ul. Krakowska was supposed to have a secret underground passage linking her to Wawel Castle. The king, it is also said, built her a palace in Łobzów, Niepolomice or Bochotnica, depending on who is telling the story. The king always protected the Jews, hence their choosing to live in a suburb near Wawel.

Below: One of the paintings displayed in the Old Synagogue Museum.

Stradom

From 1815 to 1846 only 'assimilated' immigrant Jews could settle in Stradom, and by the inter-war period of the 20th century the area was nearly totally Jewish. **Ul. Dietla** was the next area to be settled by Jews. This street was built on top of a filled-in Vistula (Wisła) River tributary which became a hive of new construction. A headquarters for Jewish orphans, the **Róża Rockowa Institute**, was built here, while the **Makkabi Sports Club** specialized (with distinction) in water polo competition.

Old Kazimierz ★★★

In 1776, Jews lost the right to trade in Kraków. So from 1816, Kazimierz became the 'Jewish area'. At one stage Kazimierz, that gorgeous cobbled jumble of houses, alleyways, synagogues and Jewish restaurants and today probably the most atmospheric suburb of Kraków, was an island in the middle of the **Vistula River**. Founded by **Kazimierz (the Great)** in 1335, it was defensively walled and had four gates – a completely separate town to Kraków. **Woollen cloth** was the key industry, while the most popular paper of the time, *The New Daily*, was printed at No. 7 ul. Orzeszkowa.

In 1927 the **Bet Jakow** or Orthodox Teachers' Seminary (for girls to study Torah) was opened at No. 10 Św. Stanisław. This was a revolutionary move. 'A spark kindled in Kraków,' they said, 'and grew to a flame that radiated throughout Poland and across the oceans.'

Above: *A tombstone at Remu Cemetery.*

Plac Wolnica ★

This square in suburban Kazimierz used to be almost as big and busy as Kraków's Main Square. Today it is a rather drab slab of concrete flanked by tree-lined sidewalks, restaurants and fruit sellers. The most impressive building is the Baroque-capped four-storey **Ethnographic Museum**, formerly the Town Hall and at one stage a state elementary school for Jewish children. The local Health Service now operates where the former **Jewish Hospital** in ul. Skawińska 8 used to be, while No. 7 ul. Bocheńska used to be the **Jewish Theatre**.

High Synagogue ★★

At one stage Jews entering Kraków had to pay a toll outside the parish school and had to pay the Catholic pupils there a fee or *Kozubalec*. All Jews also had to pay a proportion of their profits to keep the eternal flame burning in the High Synagogue (ul. Josepha 38). In 1884 the old building was pulled down and replaced with a three-storey building that sits four-square, facing a cobbled street, car park and church. Inside there is probably the best **Jewish book and music shop** in Kraków, while there is a series of restaurants the length of the street including tiny hole-in-the-wall (four tables) *pierogi* dumpling establishments. Originally built in

> ### JEWISH WEDDING
>
> The festive Clu Pub in Szeroka Square, Kazimierz, with its railings of old bicycles welded together, looks out over a square, low-fenced garden. This unprepossessing garden has a legend all of its own.
>
> Hundreds of years ago a huge wedding was held here facing the Remu (New) Synagogue and its walled old cemetery. It was a Friday. The festivities went on and on, everyone forgetting that it was now Shabbat, the Holy Day. The Rabbi tried to warn them, but it was too late. An earthquake swallowed up the whole party. The plot is to this day undeveloped.

Above: *Oskar Schindler's factory where hundreds of Jews worked.*

1563, it is called the High Synagogue, not because of its building height but because the prayer room is high above ground for safety reasons, the synagogue being close to a very rowdy town gate.

Old Synagogue ★★★

From the restaurant on the cobbled street at the corner of Jósefa and Szeroka, you overlook the old brick synagogue, square and solid in the Jewish style. One side has a railing in which Stars of David are interwoven. It overlooks a small garden. The interior of the synagogue is now a **Museum of Jewish Culture**. You pay a little to get in and, as with all the Jewish monuments in Kraków, the assistance given is exceptionally gracious.

It is the oldest standing synagogue in Poland. Basically Renaissance, its foundations are Gothic, possibly from 1407, the first in Kazimierz. The lower floor is below street level, which was vital at the time to enable the synagogue to blend in and be protected by the medieval fortifications. It became the religious and administrative centre for the whole of Kraków's Jewish community.

Two slim **Tuscan columns** built in 1570 support the roof, while between them there is a filigree iron-canopied **Bimah**, or raised reading platform.

The Old Synagogue played the role in the Jewish community that a cathedral does in Christian communities. In the sunken approach courtyard there is a marble statue erected to remember the 30 Polish citizens killed here by the Nazis in 1943.

Szeroka Square: Kazimierz ★★★

Szeroka is actually a cobbled street, but it looks like a square; it was the heart of the Jewish community. Strolling around it evokes memories of the hectic Jewish market it once was, and one can imagine the chickens, ducks, dogs, children, voices shouting, Klezmer music, hot food, cart handlers calling to make way, jugglers, haggling, arguments, women in shawls, and men in long coats and black hats.

It's not all that different now. But today, it is Israeli teenage tour groups, taxis, strolling couples, a police station, crowded restaurants and pavement pubs, and the usual flash of visitors' cameras. There are at least a dozen restaurants and five pensions around the 'Square', including three Jewish and one Indian. It is home to the **Old Jewish Cemetery** and two synagogues and is one of the most evocative places in Kraków.

Sitting having a 'toast' (toasted cheese with gherkins) and a żywiec beer, watching the world go by here in Szeroka, becomes deliciously addictive. It is non-stop people-watching action.

Remu Synagogue ★★★

Dating back to 1553, this little synagogue and its old walled cemetery made from fragments of tombstones is today the centre of Jewish religious life in Kraków, and the only active prayer house in the city. Jews from around the world come here to pray and place little stones on the graves of renowned Kraków rabbis (teachers). Men will be offered a *yarmulka* cap if they do not have a hat and, unlike at many churches, photography is not a problem. Remu Synagogue was founded by **Izrael ben Jósef**, Chief Rabbi. During the Nazi occupation of 1939–45, the synagogue was used to store rubberized body bags.

There is a wonderful wall mosaic at Remu Cemetery. It is made up of hundreds of pieces of old tombstones, many covered with Hebrew writing and period motifs of Jewish burial symbolism. It is now called the **Wailing Wall**, as so much of Jewish life in Kraków was destroyed. Auschwitz is not far away.

Buried here at Remu are **Izaak Landau**, Chief Rabbi 1754–68, **Golda** (1552), and **Izaak the Rich** (1586). There are six other synagogues in the Kazimierz area.

KOSHER

If it's kosher, it is appropriate, real, honest, guaranteed. To be kosher, pork (because of tapeworm), and shellfish (which can be poisonous) must be avoided. And there is a very specific ritual for the slaughter and removal of blood from meat, which also must always be separated from milk. Food is often interwoven into religion: Hindu cattle may not be killed; bread and wine are used for the sacrificed Body and Blood of Jesus; meat comes from animals killed with the blood drained as in Islamic Halaal custom. In Jewish custom, food not prepared in accordance with the Torah or not killed humanely is considered to be *treifah* or 'torn'.

Above: *The Cloth Hall dominates Market Square.*

BAD OLD DAYS

1200 Earthquake. There were five altogether in Kraków in historical times.
1241 Mongolian invasion.
1305 Fire destroys Wawel Cathedral.
1652 Some 24,000 die of plague (plague struck Kraków 36 times).
1772, 1793, 1795 Poland invaded and partitioned between Russia, Prussia and Austria.
1787 Locust invasion.
1850 Two monasteries, four churches and 160 houses are destroyed in the great 10-day fire.
1939 Hitler invades Poland.
1941 First Jewish ghetto in Podgórze.
1945 On 18 January the Soviet army 'liberates' Poland.
1997 Major floods.

Galicia Jewish Museum ★★
This multimedia museum at 18 Dajwór Street should be seen by every visitor to Kraków. It exists to commemorate the victims of the Shoah – the **Holocaust**, Germany's eradication of a people in Poland. It is far from being a mere record of cruelty. It is there to celebrate the fabulous Jewish culture of Galicia – the Jewish past in Poland. Galicia is that region of east-central Europe on the northern side of the Carpathians, covering southeastern Poland and the Ukraine, where so many Jews had their homes. You will seldom in Kraków receive such a warm welcome. The Jews of Europe, it seems, have gone beyond suffering and memory to a gentle state of fraternity. You hear it, you feel it, you see it. It is as if the whole of Kazimierz is hallowed ground. Tread softly, friend.

During Kraków's **Jewish Culture festival** in June each year, the Galicia Museum is open daily from 09:00 until the last visitor. There is an entrance fee but all events are free of charge unless otherwise stated. These could include the poetry of Yehuda Amichai, tram tours of Jewish Kraków, lessons in Polish for beginners, and lectures by the Department of Jewish Studies, Jagiellonian University. From 18:00 onwards during 'Shalom on Szeroka' (the final concert of the festival), entry to the Galician Jewish Museum is free all night. The coffee shop is open all day and the bookshop stocks 1400 titles.

There are over 18 Jewish 'traces of memory' sites in Old Kazimierz.

In the Ghetto
A wavy wall, not unlike a series of *matsevot* (or Jewish tombstones) – grey-blasted, humped up with snow –

stands not far from the Emalia factory made famous by Mr
Schindler (*Schindler's List*). It holds back the last crumbling
tenements of the Kraków ghetto. There were once several
gates into the ghetto, a hospital for infectious diseases,
Felix Dziuba's Optical factory, a prison, orphanage, synagogue, a confectionary factory, two German police
stations and three Nazi execution sites.

Before the outbreak of World War II, there were 65,000
Jews in Kraków, mainly in Kazimierz, Stradom and
Podgórze. From December 1939, all Jews over the age of
14 had to wear a white armband with the star of David on
it. They were banned from public transport and from
entering parks or public places. About 20ha (50 acres) in
Podgórze suburb on the banks of the Vistula was chosen
as the ghetto – 15 streets, 320 buildings. The area pre-
viously housed 3000 people, but now 16,000 refugees
(eventually 22,000) were packed in.

In 1941, Dr Jost Walbaum demanded a list of all young
women aged 14–25, to be used in scientific 'anthropologi-
cal' medical research. Only death ended their terrors. By
1942 the first deportations to the death camps, using cattle
trucks, began. About 7000 people were sent to Belżec for
killing, some 600 shot in the streets en route. In December
1942 Jews were forbidden to walk along the streets bordering the Aryan side. On 13 March 1943, 1000 Jews
were gunned down in the streets leading to Plac Zgody –
children and mothers who had refused to abandon their
children (all children under four had to be there). The surviving 3000 ghetto inhabitants were immediately shipped
to Auschwitz-Birkenau for gassing. By September the
ghetto was no more.

Fighting Wing

Many Polish gentiles did much to help the Jews. Irena
Sendler, for one, smuggled countless children out of the
Warsaw ghetto.Contrary to popular myth, the Jews also
stood and fought. **ZOB**, the Jewish fighting underground –
mainly young Zionists who later forged the state of Israel –
regularly raided the Nazis. Members of the Polish
Workers' Party organized a Resistance Group called

SUMMA CUM LAUDE

Queen Jadwiga, daughter of
King Kazimierz the Great, was
determined to restore the great
Kraków centre of learning that
fell into disuse when the king
died without a will in 1370.
She bequeathed all her
property for the restoration of
the university. The so-called
Dom Pęcherzów or **House of
Blisters**, the site of the Jewish
ghetto, was bought with her
money. **Collegium Maius**, part
of the **Jagiellonian University**
(named after Jadwiga's
husband), developed around
the Pęcherzów tenement.
Ironically, women were not
allowed to go to university
during Queen Jadwiga's time.

Above: *Floriańska Gate attracts street artists.*
Opposite: *The entrance arch at Auschwitz.*

BITTER MEMORIES

Pope Benedict's visit to Poland in May 2006 saw 900,000 attend mass on Kraków's vast Błonie Meadow. This was followed by the German-born pope's visit to Auschwitz-Birkenau, administration centre for Hitler's death camps in Poland. Alone and walking, he passed under the infamous gate, *Arbeit mach frei* ('work makes you free'). He was then escorted to the flower-bedecked death wall where inmates were regularly shot. He visited cell 18 where martyr Maximilian Kolbe (*see panel, page 57*) was imprisoned. He spoke to survivors in French, Polish and German.

Iskra or 'Spark'. In September 1942 the two organizations united and carried out numerous acts of sabotage including the highly successful attack of 22 December 1942 on Kraków's Cyganeria Café, a favourite meeting point for German officers.

The Good German

Factory owner **Herr Oskar Schindler** – war profiteer, lover of women and good brandy, wheeler dealer and hedonist – saved hundreds of persecuted Jews from the Nazi gas chambers. In charge of forced labour at Płaszów Camp was Haupsturmführer Amon Goeth, later hanged from a gibbet in Auschwitz from where he had hanged so many himself. Time and again Schindler outwitted the SS to the extent of saving his final 1000 workers by getting them out of Poland on the pretence that they were vital to the Reich's war effort. When Germany collapsed, his Jewish workers fashioned a ring for him made from gold extracted from the mouth of one of his own *Schindlerjuden*.

Schindler was declared a 'Righteous Person' by the State of Israel, an extraordinary honour. Germany awarded him the Cross of Merit and the Vatican, the Papal Knighthood of St Sylvester. He is buried in Jerusalem.

AROUND KRAKÓW
Auschwitz-Birkenau

Located near **Oświęcim**, a small industrial town, is the State Museum Auschwitz-Birkenau. (They are separated by 2km/1.25 miles). It was the Nazis' pivotal concentration and death camp, a scene of genocide on an industrial scale and the world's largest cemetery. For it was here and in a complex of 40 other camps that some two million people were systematically exterminated by the SS, 90% Jews. It lies 77km (48 miles) west of Kraków and was set up in June 1940, the first inmates being Polish political detainees, others academics, students and children rounded up randomly as a warning to others. German manufacturers relocated to Auschwitz to make use of the slave labour. Nearby Birkenau was constructed in the autumn of 1941, initially to accommodate Soviet POWs. Most died that winter. By January

1942, Hitler and his Nazis had decided on the 'Final Solution'. Poison gas was to be used to eradicate the prisoners. Birkenau (or Auschwitz II) with its space, railway and factory flow-through conditions, was constructed as a state-of-the-art murder machine.

Auschwitz

Arbeit macht frei, the cynical iron-etched sign reads over the pillbox and barbed wire entrance to Auschwitz. 'Work makes you free'. Two million people were brutalized, taken from their homes, lied to, bullied, laughed at, hair shorn, kicked, shouted at, valuables stolen, stripped in freezing snow: men, women and children. Two million is a statistic. But each one of these two million souls was a person who lived, loved, had family, enjoyed a job, a laugh with friends. Sala Garncarz Kirschner, a Polish Jew, was one such. She survived being shunted through five Nazi labour camps. She kept all her (forbidden) letters. 'Live for us for 120 years', she was encouraged in Yiddish, but in her diary she wrote: 'How do I say goodbye ... I tried to keep a smile on my face ... though my eyes were filled with tears.'

The **Auschwitz State Museum** today is Auschwitz as it always was. It is divided into double-storey block after grey block separated by the fences of once electrified barbed wire. Extermination of European Roma is one section. Then Gas Chamber, Crematorium, Collective Gallows (a length of railtrack girder), SS Garages, Death Wall, Storehouse for Zyclon B, and the Sterilization Experimental Section. The names are terrifying. Fresh flowers are placed each day in the mouth of the two side-by-side crematoriums. In Auschwitz, even school groups fall silent in the face of such malignant horror. Auschwitz-Birkenau is arguably the most moving experience you will have in Poland.

HÄFTLING NO. 16670

This was the number given to Prisoner **Raymond Maximilian Kolbe** when on 28 May 1941 he was deported to Auschwitz Concentration Camp for being Polish, and above all for being a Franciscan priest.

In the summer of 1941 three Auschwitz Häftling (prisoners), probably Polish, escaped from the Landwirtschafts Kommando (workforce). Ten prisoners were picked to die in revenge. One cried out: 'My poor wife, my children. I'll never see them again,' whereupon Kolbe stepped forward and offered to take his place. After two weeks in the starvation cell, only Kolbe was alive. The cell was needed for other victims. So the Germans injected carbolic acid into his arm. Maximilian Kolbe was beatified and his story spread worldwide.

Around Kraków

(map labels) OJCÓW NATIONAL PARK; Michałowice; 794; E77; 7; Krzeszowice; 776; 79; 951; Libiąż; Babice; Zalas; Alwernia; KRAKÓW; 780; Nadwiślański Etnographic Museum Park; Salt Mine; Oświęcim; Wisła; Skawina; Wieliczka; 7; Auschwitz-Birkenau; 949; Zator; Spytkowice; Radziszów; Brzączowice; 12.5 km; 953; 52; E77; 967; J Dobczyckie; Wadowice; Kalwaria Zebrzydowska; Izdebnik; 955; 6.25 miles

Birkenau (Brzezinka)

Birkenau lies on a huge flat plain covering 175ha (425 acres). Three hundred rat-infested wooden cabins in bleak drab rows stretch to the grey, treeless horizon. Many were burnt down by the fleeing Nazis, trying to disguise what they had done. The prison population numbered 200,000.

A railway arm leads up to the Romanesque-like tower entrance. It was on these trains, thinking they were going to be 'resettled', that the Jewish victims arrived. Two thousand people at a time were encouraged to 'have a shower'. Death from the Zyklon B cyanide gas came in 15–20 minutes. Efficiently, gold tooth fillings and personal jewellery would be removed and hair shorn (to make tailor's lining). Smooth-running electric lifts rapidly hoisted the bodies to the ovens for cremation. The incinerators and wooden funeral pyres naturally had to work overtime. Human ashes were used as fertilizer. Nothing was wasted. Children suffered the same fate as adults, although twins and the handicapped were kept aside for medical experiments. Nine thousand people, sometimes as many as 17,000, could be 'processed' in a day.

Wieliczka ★★★

Located only 15km (10 miles) southeast of Kraków is Wieliczka. Its **salt mine**, one of the oldest mines in Europe, is so unusual that it has been listed as a Unesco World Heritage Site. There are nine levels and 300km (186 miles) of tunnels, a chapel, chambers, pitfaces and galleries. Due to its special and healthy microclimate it even has a sanatorium 211m (692ft) underground. Part of the mine is a museum constructed out of beautifully lit and hand-hewn solid salt.

The Nazis manufactured aircraft parts in Wieliczka's depths during World War II. Disaster nearly struck in September 1992 when a vagabond river poured into the mine causing sinkages in the nearby town and threatening the railway link to Kraków. Five years later a halt was called to the mining but salt, extracted from the flood waters, was still sufficient to feed Poland. It is tourism, however, that now keeps Wieliczka alive. The **Blessed Kinga's Chapel**, 12m (40ft) high at a depth of 135m (443ft) and 50m (164ft) long, is a fairyland. It took 30 years to complete. Everything is carved out of salt: altarpieces, chandeliers, stairs; 20,000 tons of salt was removed to make the chapel which has also been used as both a banqueting hall and venue for classical concerts. The acoustics are fabulous. All the salt, incidentally, has a ghostly greenish colour.

Kraków's Pyramids ★★

No, they are not Egyptian or even Aztec. But they are equally mysterious. Known as *kopce* (mounds) in Kraków – or, more archaeologically correctly, barrows – these man-made hills of earth were placed over a prehistoric tomb (we surmise). The two oldest are that of **King Krakus** (mythological founder of Kraków) in Podgórze district, and **Kopiec Wandy** in Nowa Huta, Kraków's largest and ugliest urban sprawl 10km (6 miles) east of the city. Nowa Huta was built with a total lack of imagination in the Communist era to house steelworkers. The mill engineers ignored the water situation and caused major environmental pollution to Kraków.

Both Krakus and Kopiec Wandy are about 15m (50ft) high. The Krakus Mound is the scene of the 'Rekawka' games when teams dressed as knights in chain mail, horsehair plumed helmets and Viking shields do less than mortal combat to the cheers of onlookers seated up on the mound. The mounds were, of course, used as observation and strong points in pre-Christian times, around the 7th century.

Kraków is still mound-making. At least, it was up until the 1820s when the **Kościuszko Mound** was built to honour Tadeusz Kościuszko, American War of Independence hero and victor of the Racławice Partitions war in 1794 against the Russians. The mound, which you can walk up on a spiral path, is 34m (112ft) high. It was built by thousands of volunteers. The view of the city from the windy top is spectacular.

Ethnic Park ★★

The little town of **Babice**, 44km (27m) from Kraków en route to Auschwitz, has a secret: the Nadwiślański ethnographic museum-park. In a grassy area of 5ha (12 acres) in the lea of medieval Lipowiec Castle is a beautiful collection of old wooden houses and a church, a Skansen, typical of peasant folk of western Kraków. Here you will see an old oil mill, smithy, vicarage, granary, well and peasant cottages from a dozen different rural locations. The tiny church – once again all wood, including the tiles – with its onion bulb belfry is exquisite. There is also a long 1730 farmhouse or 'court' typical of the squirearchy, all period furnished.

The museum holds several special events including a knights' tournament, the 'Holiday of Honey', a regional cooking competition and something rather ambiguously titled the 'Traditional Indulgence Event'.

A steep decked walk up the forested hill takes you to **Lipowiec Castle**. It used to be the seat of the Bishops of Kraków and later a prison for clergy. The panoramic view from the round stone tower down onto a kaleidoscope of autumn-coloured trees and beyond to the Vistula and the Beskidy Mountains is truly glorious. Inside there is a historical museum.

Ojców National Park ★★

There are 700 types of mushroom in **Ojców National Park**, plus the racoon-dog, badger, wild boar, roe deer, 120 species of bird, and an incredible total of 11,000 living creatures in the lovely valleys, forests, caves and stark limestone cliffs of this unique wilderness. Even the bones of lion and cave bear have been discovered. Lying a mere 25km (16 miles) north of Kraków, the park covers an area of 1950ha (4800 acres) and boasts the most ancient human remains yet unearthed in Poland: 120,000 years old. Its claim to being Jurassic is that its geography was pulverised, shifted, and lifted by massive glacial ice sheets 200 million years ago.

Ojców is a world of finger-of-God pinnacles, castles, white cliffs, forests, eagles, rivers, sunlit mountain-fringed valleys and, of course, cave bats – the logo of the park.

Ojców Castle ★★

Medieval castles with turrets, bastions and ramparts, some occupied, some abandoned, dot the landscape of this Disney-like Jura area. Ojców Castle is practically in ruins but the sturdy rock-chunk gate tower and drawbridge still guard the ancient wind-whispering foundations, approached by a steep, wooded and winding path. The old 50m (164ft) well is also still there.

A tiny café and the Pod Kazimierzem Hotel at the foot of the castle face a handsome and neatly maintained museum where you can learn all about man and animal in the park going back to the times when our ancestors wore furs, lived in caves and had no Big Brother TV.

Above: *The 14th-century Gothic tower of Pieskowa Castle, one of a series built by war-troubled Kazimierz the Great.*

Magnificent Pieskowa ★★★

From Ojców Castle, drive past the little chapel built literally on a river, water flowing below, and then keep asking directions as you wind your way northwest through valleys and hills (a 15-minute ride, about 8km/5 miles) to Pieskowa Castle. Beyond **Hercules's Club**, a 20m (66ft) giant stalagmite of limestone rock, **Pieskowa Skała Castle** looms huge across the frozen valley. It is largely Renaissance in style and red-roofed. It has nine connected structures, some eight storeys high, and four towers hovering over the snow-forested cliff and river far below. The multistoreyed multiarcaded courtyard leads to the superb many-roomed **Museum of European Art** (14th to 19th centuries). The colourful and busy displays of furniture, paintings, sculptures and decor, century by century, are stunning, and more intimate and accessible than **Wawel Museum** of which it is an adjunct.

Kraków at a Glance

BEST TIMES TO VISIT

The weather in Europe can be either cold, hot, wet or windy, and the key to choosing the best time to visit is to go when it is not excessively so. Spring and autumn are the only times when the weather is comparable with such benign climes as those of California, Chile or the African highveld, and then, in Poland, it is perfect. In **high summer**, with average temperatures of 24°C (75°F) from June through to August, Poland has plenty of sunshine. But this is when the whole of Europe comes out to play. In Kraków's Gothic churches you risk being swamped by teenage tour groups, while the more popular Baltic beaches leave little room for a quiet read. **Spring**, when the lovely wilderness flowers bloom, particularly in the Tatra mountains and across the Mazuria Lakeland, is the ideal hiking and sailing season. **Autumn**, which lasts from September to mid-October, is the best time to travel around the country and it is also the season of many cultural activities. But in mid-October it can be comfortably warm one day and suddenly snow the next. **Winters** are bitter, the winds Siberian, blanketing much of the country in snow for up to three months. But this, of course, is winter sports time

in the panoramic, if at times over-stretched, Tatra mountain resorts around Zakopane in the south of the country.

GETTING THERE

By Air: There are regular scheduled and cut-cost flights from many European cities to Kraków and Warsaw, especially from Germany, Ireland, the UK, France and Russia. Flying time from London to Kraków is approximately two hours 30 minutes. There are no direct flights to Kraków from South Africa, Australia or New Zealand. The John Paul II International Airport is at Balice, 15km (10 miles) from Kraków, and is served by plenty of metered taxis. BA and Aer Lingus operate direct flights from London Gatwick and Dublin to Kraków, while LOT Polish Airlines fly direct to Warsaw from Heathrow, Dublin, Manchester and Chicago. The low-cost airlines are battling due to fuel costs. Scheduled flights have also decreased since the worldwide fuel crisis.

By Bus: International buses arrive at the new terminal on ul. Bosacka, behind the railway station. Contact Eurolines, tel : 0870 514 3219. Buses take much longer than flying and are not necessarily all that much cheaper.

By Car: From London, count on two days' driving on busy motorways through Belgium,

Germany and the Czech Republic to reach Kraków. Polish roads are not as good as those in Western Europe. The distance is 1700km (1056 miles). Drive on the right. No handheld mobiles allowed. Carry your licence; non-EU citizens should carry an international licence.

By Rail: This is a more expensive option than going by air. You can take the Eurostar to Brussels and then to Berlin and Kraków (changing in Berlin). To book online, try Trainseurope, tel: (UK) 0900 195 0101, www.trainseurope.co.uk or Deutsche Bahn, tel: (UK) 08702 435 363, www.deutsche-bahn.co.uk The Orient Express now visits Kraków after an absence of 25 years. It is exotically nostalgic (Agatha Christie) and luxurious. Individual or double sleeper compartments, as on any trains in Europe, push the price right up.

By Sea: There are regular ferry services between Gdańsk and Gydnia to and from Sweden and Denmark. The ferry takes around 10–18 hours. Bringing your car will cost about 150% of the passenger fare. Discount is available for senior citizens and students.

Package Tours: A three-night Kraków city break including flights and three-star accommodation costs around

Kraków at a Glance

US$625 from London. Guided tour packages, say for seven days, would cost around US$1550. Try Polorbis, tel: 48 20 7636 2217, www.polorbis.co.uk

GETTING YOUR BEARINGS

Poland lies between Germany (not far from Berlin) and Eastern Europe, with a 450km (280-mile) stretch of Baltic coastline in the north and the Tatra mountains (great for skiing) in the south. Warsaw is located in the middle of the country, Kraków in the south and Gdańsk (known as Danzig in German days) in the north. There are fascinating old historic centres, or *stare miasto* as they are known in Poland, in most towns.

GETTING AROUND

From the Airport: The train station is only a few hundred metres from Kraków's smart little airport. Trains run every 30 minutes – from 04:24 until just after midnight – to Kraków's Central Station at a cost of 4zł per person. Bus No. 192 also takes you to the Central Station. A metered taxi – there are plenty just outside the airport exit – costs approximately 70zł, and is probably the best choice for your first time in Kraków.
Walking in Kraków: Walking is the best way to explore Kraków. If you are staying in or near the Old City or

Kazimierz, get your north-south bearings, collect a little map from your hotel (or use our map at the back of this book), get a bottle of water and some local cash from an ATM, carry an umbrella and walk. (You can jaywalk but its best not to and cars drive on the right so keep an eye over your left shoulder when crossing roads.) If you are from the UK or any country where one keeps to the left, remember that in Poland it's the other way round. People on a pavement, for example, will always tend to approach and pass you on your left. If you stick to the left, you'll end up continually bumping into people.
By Tram: Trams are the main mode of transport in Polish cities. They operate from 05:00–23:00. Buy the tickets from any newspaper kiosk. On boarding, cancel your ticket in the little metal box. These same tickets can be used on city buses, with the same cancelling procedure. In general the facilities for disabled travellers are not very good. Notices on trams forbid six things; these

include eating ice cream and blowing trumpets – and all unsociable activities in between. Trams are crowded at rush hour with long – but orderly – queues. Pick-pockets favour these times.
By Car: Kraków city is divided into three parking zones. Zone A, which incorporates the Main Market Square and surrounding access streets, is closed to motorized traffic; walking or bicycles only are permitted here. Zone B, the Planty Park green belt that surrounds Kraków, has parking available in designated areas from 10:00–18:00 but it is, of course, further to walk to the main sights. Zone C, outside the Planty green lung, can also be used for parking from 10:00–18:00.
By Train Around Poland: This is the best way to travel. It is very inexpensive, even first class. From Kraków to Warsaw the journey is two hours and 45 minutes by express train. And it takes just eight hours to Gdańsk, the furthest point north. Reservations are essential for the Fast Intercity trains (marked 'IC' in red on

KRAKÓW	J	F	M	A	M	J	J	A	S	O	N	D
MAX TEMP °C	0	1	7	13	20	22	24	23	19	14	6	3
MIN TEMP °C	-5	-5	-1	3	9	12	15	14	10	5	1	-2
MAX TEMP °F	32	34	45	55	67	72	76	73	66	56	44	37
MIN TEMP °F	22	22	30	38	48	54	58	56	49	42	33	28
RAINFALL mm	28	28	35	46	46	94	111	91	62	49	37	36
RAINFALL in	1.1	1.1	1.4	1.8	1.8	3.7	4.4	3.6	2.4	1.9	1.5	1.4

timetables). You can travel cross country for less than US$35 (50% more if it is Express or Intercity; these trains have buffet cars and snack trolleys; the occasional compartment is for smokers only). Sleepers are available. Buying tickets at a station can take time, since few people speak English. So ask someone to write down your request in Polish on a piece of paper. Each platform has two tracks, and some carriages only go part of the way. *Odjazdy* means 'departures' and *przyjazdy* 'arrivals'. Make sure you know what you are doing, ask for help, and never arrive at the last minute.

By Bus Around Poland: Travelling by bus is not as fast as the train, but it is obligatory if visiting some of the smaller provincial towns, e.g. in the Lake District. Timetables are reliable, services wide ranging and buses (PKS) comfortable. The main bus station in many towns is often located alongside the train station. Toilets are available (have your coins ready) at main bus stations, but seldom on buses.

LUXURY

Copernicus Hotel, ul. Kanonicza 16, tel: (012) 424 3400, e-mail: copernicus@ hotel.com.pl website: www.hotel.com.pl Cream-of-the-crop hotel with 29 rooms. Historic building between Old Market and Wawel Castle. Superb service. Wall frescoes, marble and terrace views of Wawel.

Amadeus, ul. Mikołajska 20, tel: (012) 429 6070, e-mail: amadeus@janpol.com.pl website: www.hotel-amadeus.pl This hotel has 20 rooms and is Prince Charles's favourite. It was inspired (naturally) by the era of Mozart.

Qubus Hotel, ul. Nadwiślańska 6, tel:(012) 374 5100, e-mail: krakow@ qubushotel.com website: www.qubushotel.com There are 194 rooms in this modern business hotel. Broadband Internet, swimming pool, fitness centre.

Grand Hotel, ul. Sławkowska 5, tel: (012) 421 7255, e-mail: hotel@grand.pl website: www.grand.pl This hotel has 62 rooms and nine suites. Joseph Conrad and Margaret Thatcher both stayed here. It is as grand as its name.

Gródek, ul. Na Gródku 4, tel: (012) 431 9030, e-mail: grodek@donimirski.com website: www.donimirski. com The Gródek has 23 rooms and the ambience is romantic.

Pod Róża, ul. Floriańska 14, tel: (012) 424 3300, website: www.hotelcom.pl There are 57 rooms, two restaurants. Franz Liszt stayed here. Filled with antiques.

Elektor, ul. Szpitalna 28, tel: (012) 423 2317, e-mail: elektor@hotelelektor.com.pl website: www.hotelelektor. com.pl Elegant, sumptuous, with 21 de luxe rooms.

Francuski, ul. Pjarska 13, tel: (012) 627 3737, e-mail: francuski@orbis.pl website: www.orbisonline.pl This hotel has 42 rooms, smart gold-braided doormen and classical furniture.

Radisson SAS, ul. Straszewskiego 17, tel: (012) 618 8888, e-mail: krakow@ radissonsas.com website: www.radissonsas.com New, up-market hotel, 196 rooms. Works of art on the walls. Heated bathroom floors.

Ostoya Palace Hotel, ul. Piłsudskiego 24, tel: (012) 430 9000, e-mail: ostoya@ mpoczta.net website: www.ostoyapalace.pl The Ostoya Palace has 24 rooms. *Fin de siècle* elegance, Jacuzzis.

Stary, ul. Szczepańska 5, tel: (012) 384 0808, e-mail: stary@hotel.com.pl website: www.stary.hotel.com.pl There are 53 rooms. Super luxurious – deep pocket guests only.

MID-RANGE

Atrium, ul. Krzyna 7, tel: (012) 430 0203, e-mail: hotelatrium@hotelatrium.pl website: www.hotelatrium. com.pl The Atrium has 52 rooms, suites have kitchenettes. Nordic style.

Chopin Hotel Cracow, ul. Przy Rondzie 2, tel: (012)

Kraków at a Glance

299 0000, e-mail: info@chopinhotel.pl website: www.chopinhotel.com Modern, functional hotel with 220 rooms; good value.

Hotel Pollera, ul. Szpitalna 30, tel: (012) 422 1044, e-mail: rezerwacja@pollera.com.pl website: www.pollera.com.pl There are 45 rooms. Flower box windowsills, five minutes' walk from main Market Square. Polish cuisine.

Fortuna Bis, ul. Piłsudskiego 25, tel:(012) 430 1025, e-mail: infobis@hotel-fortuna.com.pl website: www.hotel-fortuna.com.pl This hotel has 23 rooms. Courtyard balcony. African restaurant.

Hotel Europejski, ul. Lubicz 5, tel: (012) 423 2510, e-mail: he@he.pl website: www.he.pl There are 48 rooms; ask for a room over-looking the main courtyard. Near the station.

Amber, ul. Gabarska 10, tel: (012) 421 0606, e-mail: office@hotel-amber.pl web-site: www.hotel-amber.pl The Amber has 18 rooms. There is satellite TV. Located on a quiet street.

Hotel Alexander, ul. Gabarska 18, tel: (012) 422 9660, e-mail: biuro@alexhotel.pl website: www.alexhotel.pl There are 40 rooms, plus a conference room with a good view of the old city.

Senacki, ul. Grodzka 51, tel: (012) 422 7686, e-mail: recepcja@senacki.krakow.pl

website: www.senacki.krakow.pl The Senacki has 20 rooms. Excellent value in a historic and now renovated old building in the old city.

Floryan, ul. Floriańska 38, tel: (012) 431 1418, e-mail: floryan@floryan.com.pl website: www.floryan.com.pl There are 21 rooms; decor is colourful, modern and tasteful.

BUDGET

Royal, ul. Św Gertrudy 26–29, tel: (012) 421 3500, e-mail: hotel@royal.com.pl website: www.royal.com.pl The Royal has 111 rooms and is located in a beautiful setting with view on a park.

Hotel Pod Wawelem, Pl. Na Gróblach 22/cnr Powiśle, tel: (012) 426 2626, e-mail: rezerwacja@hotelpod.pl website: www.hotelpodwawelem.pl There are 47 rooms in this popular hotel in a choice location opposite Wawel Castle.

Dom Polonii, Rynek Główny 14 (Floor 3), tel: (012) 428 0406, e-mail: biuro@swp.Krakow.pl website: www.wspolnota-polska.krakow.pl A small hotel – three rooms only – in the heart of the Old Quarter.

The Piano Guest House, ul. Katowa 4, tel: (012) 632 1371, website: www.katowa4.com This guest-house, owned by a pianist, has ten rooms. The decor is arty, with flowers and antiques. It has a garden.

Wawel Tourist, ul. Poselska 22, tel: (012) 424 1300, website: www.wawel-tourist.com.pl There are 15 rooms. It is located just south of Market Square. Nothing too fancy, but friendly.

Good Bye Lenin Hostel, ul. Berka Joselewicza 31–031, tel: (012) 421 2030, e-mail: krakow@goodbyelenin.pl website: www.goodbyelenin.pl A choice of double rooms and dorms. A great backpackers' option, with free breakfast, free linen, free laundry, multilingual staff. There is a garden with BBQ facilities.

Trecius, ul. Św. Tomasza 18, tel: (012) 421 2521, website: www.trecius.krakow.pl Eight rooms, right in the heart of the old city. Every room is different.

Rubens, ul. Rejtana 5, tel: (012) 423 5834, website: www.hotel-rubens.pl This establishment has ten rooms. It is housed in a 100-year-old restored building, with flowers and paintings – though not by Rubens!

Klezmer Huis, ul. Szeroka 6, tel: (012) 411 1245, e-mail: klezmer@klezmer.pl web-site: www.klezmer.pl Ten rooms in an old building that was once a ritual Jewish bathing house or *mikveh*.

Kazimierz

This is the old Jewish area of Kraków, with synagogues, tiny cobbled streets, and also a number of restaurants.

LUXURY
Rubinstein, ul. Szeroka 12, tel: (012) 384 0000, e-mail: recepeja@hotelrubinstein. com website: www.hotel rubinstein.com This hotel has 27 rooms. Carved wood finishings, antiques.

MID-RANGE
Karmel, ul. Kupa 15, tel: (012) 430 6697, e-mail: hotel@karmel.com.pl website: www.karmel.com.pl There are ten rooms here, and a good Italian restaurant.
Alef, ul. Szeroka 17, tel: (012) 421 38 70, website: www.alef.pl Four apartment rooms on Szeroka Square. Charming restaurant with live Klezmer Jewish music.
Eden, ul. Cienna 15, tel: (012) 430 6565, e-mail: eden@hoteleden.pl website: www.hoteleden.pl The Eden has 27 rooms. It caters particularly for American Jewish guests. It is housed in a 15th-century building. The welcome brochure, strangely, is a list of hotel regulations.
Ester, ul. Szeroka 20, tel: (012) 429 1188, e-mail: biuro@hotel-ester.krakow.pl website: www.hotel-ester. krakow.pl This hotel has 32 rooms. Good restaurant.
Astoria, ul. Józefa 24, tel: (012) 617 6410, e-mail: biuro@astoriahotel.pl website: www.astoriahotel.pl There are 33 rooms. The restaurant serves Polish cuisine.

Kazimierz, ul. Miodowa 16, tel: (012) 421 6629, e-mail: hotel@hk.com.pl website: www.hk.com.pl The Kazimierz Hotel has 35 rooms and there is stained glass in the restaurant.

BUDGET
Abel, ul. Józefa 30, tel: (012) 411 8736, e-mail: hotelabel@hotelabel.pl website: www.hotelabel.pl There are 15 simple rooms in this three-storey corner house. The hospitality here is magical. Cellar pub. Recommended.

WHERE TO EAT

Polish
Kawiarnia u Zalipianek, ul. Szewska 24, near Planty Park, tel: (012) 422 2950. Seats 140. This restaurant is open 10:00–22:00 every day. It serves 'Zalipia' Polish country cuisine and has a folksy hand-painted interior plus green pavement café. Hostess soup.
Pod Baranem, ul. Św Gertrudy 21, tel: (012) 429 4022. Seats 60. Open 10:00–23:00. Home-style cooking, marinated hams, smoked catfish on Fridays, hare pâté, blueberry dessert.
Bar Grodski, ul. Grodska 47, tel: (012) 422 6807. Seats 150. Open 09:00–19:00. Very cheap communist-era eatery or milk bar (*bar mleczny*, or more commonly known in Kraków as *jadło-dajnia*). It has an awesome cellar, and heaped plates of fattening nosh.
Hawelka, Rynek Główny 34, Main Square, tel: (012) 422 0631. Open 11:00–23:00. Seats 100. Tuxedoed waiters in *fin de siècle* formality. Serves seafood as well as traditional game meats.
Poezja Smaku (the literal translation is 'Elegant Poetry' and in fact it is very arty), ul. Jagiellonska 5, tel: (012) 292 8020. Open 12:00–00:00. Seats 120. Connected brick-walled alcoves with busts, antiques and mirrors. Be sure to try the honeyed cheese.
Ogniem i Mieczem, Pl. Serkowskiego 7, tel: (012) 656 2328. Open 12:00–00:00. Seats 120. The restaurant's name translates as 'With Fire and Sword' after Henryk Sienkiewicz's two-volume epic of that name. It is an Asterix heaven of boar meat, ancient recipes, bear skins, and even a winged 17th-century King Sobieski cavalryman.
Once upon a Time in Kazimierz, ul. Szeroka 1, tel: (012) 421 2117. Seats 50. Open 10:00–00:00. Collectors' paradise of old knick-knacks. Serves wholesome meals.
Wierzynek, Rynek Główny 15, tel: (012) 424 9600. Seats 80. Open 13:00–00:00. Theoretically this smart restaurant goes back to 1364, or at any rate its ancestors did. Tapestries, bowtied waiters, flowers, champagne.

Kraków at a Glance

Farmona, ul. Jugowicka 10, tel: (012) 252 7070. Open 07:00–22:00. Seats 80. Celebrity chef, leather seats.

CK Dezerter, ul. Bracka 6, tel: (012) 422 7931. Seats 70. Open 11:00–23:00. Polish meats and sour soups in a cosy atmosphere.

Pod Gwiazdami, ul. Grodska 5, tel: (012) 430 2657. Open 12:00–23:00. Seats 80. The name means 'Under the Stars', because it has a glass roof. Serves European and Polish food.

Kurdish
U Ziyada, ul. Jodłowa 13, tel: (012) 429 7105.Open 10:00–00:00. Seats 100. Housed in a castle above the Vistula River.

Jewish
Klezmer-Hois, ul. Szeroka 6, tel: (012) 411 1245. Open 10:00–23:00. Seats 45. All kosher cuisine including Jewish caviar, goose liver, gefilte fish. Like a small London club. Live Jewish, Roma and Russian music.

Noah's Ark, ul. Szeroka 2, tel: (012) 429 1528. Seats 80. Open 09:00–02:00. Upstairs for live Klezmer music every evening at 20:30. Cosy atmosphere. Downstairs Jewish cuisine from Poland's Małopolska region is served.

Bagelmama, ul. Prodbrzezie 2, tel: (012) 431 1942. Seats 6–12. Open 10:00–21:00 (closed Monday).

Magnificent and imaginative bagels with delicious and exotic toppings. Basically takeaway. The word 'bagel' comes from the Polish-Yiddish *beygel*. It migrated to New York and Chicago with the vast waves of Jewish Polish immigrants in the 19th and 20th centuries and soon became the most popular 'takeout'.

Italian
Pepe Rosso, ul. Kupa 15, tel: (012) 431 0875. Seats 70. One of Kraków's very best Italian restaurants. Excellent service.

Mamma Mia, ul. Karmelicka 14, tel: (012) 430 0492. Seats 80. Open 12:00–23:00. Woodfired oven, rough brick interior. Heavenly pizzas plus much more.

Aqua e Vino Old Town, ul. Wislna 5, tel: (012) 421 2567. Open 11:00–00:00. Francesco will suggest delectable Italian dishes.

Lithuanian–Ukrainian
Jarema, Pl. Matejki 5, tel: (012) 429 3669. Seats 120. Open 11:00–23:00. The decor and cuisine hark back to the days of Polish grandeur. There are also vegetarian options.

French
Cyrano de Bergerac, ul. Sławkowska 26, Old Town, tel: (012) 411 7288. Seats 70. Open 12:00–00:00 (closed Sundays). Superb

cellar restaurant. Widely recognized.

Brazilian
Ipanema, ul. Św. Tomasza, tel: (012) 422 5323. Seats 70. Open 13:00–00:00 (because no-one gets up early in Rio). Carmen Miranda bananas, avocados and fishing nets. Also plenty of Afro touches.

Japanese
Edo Sushi, ul. Bożego Ciała 3, tel: (012) 422 2424. Seats 60. Open 12:00–22:00 (later on Friday and Saturday). Take your shoes off to enter the rice-paper-walled sushi restaurant, with mats, low tables, birdsong and many delicate dishes.

Cuban
Buena Vista, ul. Józefa 26, tel: (0) 668 035 000. Seats 70. Open 12:00–23:30. Live Cuban music on Thursdays, 1950s Havana décor. Serves the best *mojito* in town, plus hot fruit tapas, daiquiris, and *las fresas con nata*, or strawberries and cream. The atmosphere is pure Hemingway.

Seafood
Restauracja Morgan, ul. Zamoyskiego 52, tel: (012) 656 0893. Seats 120. Open 13:00–00:00. Fresh fish, lobster, tuna, salmon. There's lots of nautical décor, including navigation charts and canvas sails.

Kraków at a Glance

Vegetarian
Vega, ul. Św. Gertrudy 7, tel: (012) 422 3494, seats 70. Open 09:00–21:00. This restaurant has a view over Planty Park and a marvellous assortment of dried flower arrangements.

American
Sioux Classic, Rynek Główny 22, tel: (012) 421 3462. Open 11:00–23:00. Seats 160. Central. This lively young steak joint is pure 'John Wayne at Home on the Range'. There are branches all over Poland as the country imbibes Texas culture.

Indian
Bombaj Tandoori, ul. Szeroka 7, tel: (012) 422 3797. Seats 50. Open 12:00–23:00. Reasonable Indian cuisine is served in an intimate atmosphere.

Chinese
Czerwony Smok, ul. Podgórska 34 (Galeria Shopping Mall, Kazimierz), tel: (012) 433 0351. Open 10:00–22:00 (until 20:00 on Sunday) Seats 100. Authentic and inexpensive Chinese dishes are served here.

Mauritanian
Bulwar Kurlandzki (Vistula floating restaurant), tel: (0) 692 383 661. Seats 120. Open 11:00–00:00. Serves crêpes and rum amid lots of oil paintings and brass instruments.

Argentinian
Pimiento, ul. Józefa 26, tel: (012) 421 2502. Seats 60. Open 12:00–23:00. Excellent Argentinian beef for hungry gauchos. Open kitchen.

Condiments
In Poland salt tends to be in multi-holed dispensers and pepper in single-holed dispensers – opposite to for example the UK.

SHOPPING

Amber: Jewelry Schubert, at 13 Floriańska St, claim to be the maestro among jewellers. Open 09:00–20:00. There are other, similar shops in this street.

Arts and Crafts: Cloth Hall, Main Market. There's a bit of everything and lots of buzz.

Books/Music: Empik Megastore, Rynek Główny 5. Many Kraków bookstores offer an English selection, e.g. Massolit Books, English bookstore, Felicjanek 4, Novy Swiat.

Ceramics: Gala, Św Gertrudy 36. Colourful decorated stoneware.

Clothing: There are some amazing leather jackets and furs available at flea markets, and you can always find 'antique' collectibles. Designer jeans are for sale everywhere (and perhaps made anywhere), and you

can buy good leather shoes at reasonable prices in many a small store.

Department Stores: Galeria (shopping mall) Kazimierz will advise you to 'Polish your style'. At 34 Podgórska Street, it has 130 brand shops (open 10:00–22:00).

Glass Products: For high quality, try: Krosno/Athena, Plac Mariacki 1, or Polskie Szkło, ul. Grodzka 36.

Leather: Ston Torbalski, ul. Slawkowska 4.

Vodka: Szambelan, Gotebia 2 (via Bracka Stentrame). Vodka is originally Russian, but there are dozens of Polish varieties.

TOURS AND EXCURSIONS

Chopin Concerts: Four days a week in warmer months at 19:00, at 14 Main Market Square. Reservations tel: 48 662 007 255. Tickets also from the Tourist Information Centre, 21 Floriańska St, www.cracowforyou.pl

Communism Tours: Crazy Guides will take you in an old trusty East German Trabant car on an eccentric tour trip to the Nowa Huta steelworks and suburb, including a communist-era milk bar where you'll hear hilarious anecdotes of the 'good ol' days'. The tour is recommended for connois-

Kraków at a Glance

seurs of communism. Hotel Florian, 38 Floriańska St, tel: 488 500 091 200, e-mail: mike@crazyguides.com website: www.crazyguides.com

Bus Tours: There are several bus tours of Kraków. Try: 'Cracow City', 'Salt Mine', 'Auschwitz-Birkenau', 'Traces of Jewish Culture', 'In the Footsteps of John Paul II', and many more. Contact Cracow Tours, 3 Krupnicza St, tel: (012) 430 0726, e-mail: office@cracowtours.pl website: www.cracowtours.pl

Private Car Tours: Ojców National Park/Pieskowa Skała Castle, Black Madonna Shrine, Zakopane and Tatra Mountains, Old Jewish District (Schindler's List). Property Investment Tour. Point Travel DMC Luxury Krakówtours, Hotel Chopin, tel: (012) 461 2421 or (012) 299 0000, e-mail: kracow@krakow-tours.pl website: www.krakow-tours.pl

Bike Rental: Café Gallery Zakopianka, ul. Św. Marka 34, Planty Park, tel: (012) 421 4045 (15zł per day).

Walking Tours: Cool Tour Company, ul. Grodzka 2, tel: (0) 509 031 898. They guarantee you'll be off the beaten track and will never be bored. Tours start at 10:00 and 14:00 from Wojciecha Church.

KRAKÓW FESTIVALS

Late June/early July: Jewish Culture Festival in Kazimierz.
July: Street Theatre Festival.
August: Music in Old Kraków Festival.

USEFUL CONTACTS

City Tourist Information: ul. Floriańska 6, tel: (012) 432 0101, www.biurofestiwalowe.pl (near station).
Kraków Tourist Information Point: ul. Floriańska 6, tel: (012) 397 3624, www.seekrakow.com
Cultural Information Centre: ul. Św. Jana 2, tel: (012) 421 7787, e-mail: karnet@krakow2000.pl
Tourist Information Office: Rynek Główny 41, tel: (012) 619 2463.
Ambulance: 999.
Police: 997.
Fire: 998.
To contact an ambulance, the police or the fire brigade from a mobile phone, tel: 112.
Medical Advice: (012) 9439.
24-hour Pharmacy: ul. Kalwaryjska 94, tel: (012) 656 1850. Or Apteka, ul. Galla 26, tel: (012) 636 7365.
DHL: ul. Balicka 79, tel: 0801 34 53 45.
Airport: tel: (012) 411 1955.
British Airways: www.ba.com
Car Rental: Avis, tel: (012) 629 6108.
Radio Taxi: tel: 9191.
Express Taxi: tel: 9629.
Radio Taxi Partner: tel: 96 339 688. Taxi service for the disabled.

POLISH FESTIVALS

February: International Composers Competition, Warsaw.
April: Warsaw Ballet Days.
May: Probaltica, Baltic States Arts & Music Festival, Toruń.
Summer: Festivals in Lublin include the National Festival of Town Bugle Calls, the International Guitar Festival and the European Festival of Performing Arts.
June: Kazimierz Dolny: Folk Art Fair.
Late June: Malta International Open-air Theatre Festival, Poznań.
24 June: St John's Fair, Poznań. With live music and stalls.
1–15 August: Dominican Fair, Main Town, Gdańsk, with street theatre, craft and stalls. Also International Chamber Music Festival, same time.
August: Chopin Festival in Warsaw.
Mid-August: In the Tatra Mountains, there's a week-long Festival of Mountain Folklore and Music, where local Górale groups plus dozens of other competing European countries provide concerts and parades.
Late October: The prestigious Jazz Jamboree in Warsaw.
Winter: In Lublin, the Oldest Songs from Little Europe Festival and St Nick's Day International Folk Music Festival.
December: Christmas Cribs Competition, Czartoryski Museum, home to Leonardo da Vinci's 1482 painting *Lady with an Ermine*. (Only five cities in the world have a painting by Leonardo.)

3
Gdańsk

Land of lakes, lagoons, rivers and golden dunes and lapped by the chilly Baltic Sea, northern Poland stretches from the Russian coastal enclave of Kaliningrad in the east to the vast Polish-German lagoon of Szczecin in the west, the shallow marshy delta of the Odra or Oder River that divides the two countries – a distance of 450km (280 miles). Dunes, sea birds, lonely sea and the sky, it is Poland's seaside holiday *costa*. It is also the site of **Gdańsk** (pronounced Gdainsk), Poland's great port, home to Fahrenheit, inventor of the mercury thermometer, philosopher Arthur Schopenhauer, writer Günter Grass and the Solidarity shipyard trade union that caused the fall of communism in Poland in 1989, and ultimately that of the Soviet dictatorship throughout Europe.

Gdańsk, originally Gyddanyzc, was named after a rare pigeon found in this area by migrant Slav fishermen who settled at the mouth of the Wisła or Vistula River 1500 years ago. Written history only began in AD997 when the missionary Bishop of Prague, Adalbert, converted the local people to Catholic Christianity. Gdańsk has always been the great survivor, coveted for its combined strategic position on the Baltic and the 1090km (677-mile) long Vistula. It was fought over by Pomeranian dukes, Teutonic knights from Germany, Napoleon, Prussians, Lithuanians, Hitler and Stalin. By AD1550 Gdańsk was Poland's largest city and the greatest trading port in Eastern and Central Europe.

Gdańsk is the largest of three interlinked Baltic cities (combined population 800,000). Together with **Gydnia** and **Sopot**, they stretch 40km (25 miles) along the lovely

DON'T MISS

★★★ **Royal Way:** in the footsteps of kings.
★★★ **Town Hall:** medieval history, restaurants and buskers.
★★ **Hanseatic Merchants' Houses:** sumptuous one-upmanship.
★★ **Motława River and Bridge:** pirate ships, amber jewellery.
★★ **St Mary's Church:** from 1343; 78m (256ft) bell tower.
★★ **Solidarity Monument:** the beginning of the end of communism in Europe.
★ **Piaski:** lovely sea, sky and forest on the Russian border.

Opposite: *Golden Gate, the main entrance into the Old Town.*

Gdańsk

Gulf of Gdańsk. But it is Gdańsk that revels in fascinating history, with its medieval **Route of Kings** through its **Stare Miasto** or Old Town. Sopot is a fashionable beach resort, while Gydnia is better known for its business acumen and hi-tech port.

Royal Way ★★★

Walk through the chunky Renaissance **Upland Gate** (or **Brama Wyżynna**) at the start of the Royal Way and entrance into the town centre (or centrum miasta) and you will be following in the footsteps of warrior king Jan Sobieski, who with his winged cavalrymen rescued Vienna from the Turkish siege in 1683. The beautiful old town was laid out in the mid-14th century, reached its grain and amber-trading zenith in the 16th–18th centuries and was destroyed in World War II only to be meticulously rebuilt to what it had been 400 years earlier. This Gothic gateway (and torture house) is followed by the most impressive of the Old Town's medieval constructions, the **Golden Gate** or **Złota Brama**, so called because it is crowned with gilded statues to such lofty trading virtues as piety, reason, freedom and, of course, wealth.

Hanseatic High Street ★★

For centuries, Gdańsk was known as Danzig, the name given to it by the Teutonic Knights, the somewhat less-than-holy warriors from Germany who swept across the region 800 years ago converting the willing to Catholicism and killing the rest – normal practice in dealing with 'pagans'. The **Danzig Eastland Company** became so powerful that at

Opposite: *The Town Hall spire towers over Długa Street, the main thoroughfare of the Old Town.*

one stage its trading embrace was more omniambient than the later British East India Company that paved the way for the colonization of India. Salt, fish, hides, metals and, above all, wood were shipped and traded. Spruce (from the Polish *z Prus* or 'from Prussia') timber was a major export, as was grain from the Polish plains, while the Baltic amber trade was extant long before ancient Rome. With extraordinary wealth like this – on a par with today's financial wunderkind dealers – opulent construction proceeded apace. **Long Street** or **Ulica Długa** – actually only 500m (550yd) long – is like a dream of old Flanders or Amsterdam, with its cobbled strollway and its multicoloured, upright and Dutch-designed merchant prince townhouses.

Town Hall **

The Town Hall, the heartbeat of all medieval life, looking not unlike a seashore sand dribble castle, marks the start of **Długi Targ** or **Long Market Square** and is a marvellous spot to watch buskers dressed as pirates, ballet girls doing acrobatics and instant portrait artists flattering sitters – just as it was in medieval times, with the exception of gory executions, a favourite with the populace in days of yore. There is plenty of fast food, balloons for the children, cheap and dazzling necklaces of amber and a host of umbrella'd cafés for coffee and cheesecake.

One of the turrets on the Town Hall features a sundial with the somewhat lugubrious inscription (in Latin): 'Our days are nothing but shadow'. The great edifice is topped with a gilded helm, pinnacle and 14 bells. One room displays evocative black-and-white photos of Gdańsk in 1945, revealing a withering moonscape of the city decimated by

SCOTLAND THE TRADE

Mary Queen of Scots never actually did an all-in tour of Gdańsk, but her home in St Andrews was largely built of timber shipped to Scotland from Gdańsk. With its relaxed religious climate, trade and wealth, Gdańsk attracted many Scots. By 1600 there were 30,000 Scots in Gdańsk, mainly peddlers. A travelling salesman is still known in the local Kashubian dialect as a *szot*. Others became military mercenaries fighting Swedes, Turks and Russians. Gdańsk has two suburbs, Nowe Szkoty and Stare Szkoty (New and Old Scots) and at least two Scots pubs, albeit their Gay Gordon decor is somewhat confused with the hated Sassenach, as the Scots castigated the English.

British and American bombing and later Soviet artillery. Only the **Red Summer Council Hall**'s lush 450-year-old fittings survived the high explosives. They had fortunately been spirited away in 1942. Everything has been rebuilt with dedicated and superbly skilled restoration.

Golden Gates ★★

Neptune, mythical Roman god of the sea, has always been a favourite with seaports like Gdańsk. A monument to him stands in front of the ornate white **Artus Court**. Neptune, irritated at the wishing coins thrown in the fountain, struck them with his trident, crushing the gold into flakes that henceforth glittered in the water. Artus Court (after King Arthur of the Round Table) was the medieval office of merchant guilds. It contains the 1546 Russian 520-tiled stove, 10m (33ft) high, the world's largest. **New Bench House** next door is equally full of Dutch craftsmanship. At 13:00 look out for the blue-and-white **Hedwiga**, the 17th-century maiden (imprisoned by her uncle) as she appears wistfully at one window.

Golden House or **Złota Kamienica** is gorgeous, but it is not golden, although bits and pieces of its second choice sculptures are. The first choice plus boat were lost at sea.

The roof parapet is topped by four statues – Mayor Speymann's favourite ladies – **Cleopatra** and **Antigone** – plus **Achilles** of the weak heel and **Oedipus** who unwittingly killed his father and married his mother. Mayor Jan Speymann, who built the home in 1617 in Renaissance style, obviously had Greco-Roman taste. The house may be haunted: Speymann's wife, a benevolent ghost, wanders the corridors, whispering 'Do justice, fear nobody' – one of the maxims over the entrance.

Green Gate marks the end of both the market and the Royal Way on the edge of the **Motława River**. It is not particularly green. The style is mannerist or idiosyncratic: Dutch gables, statues, red roof, ballast-bricks, plants, moss and huge windows which, admittedly, when the light catches them, look green. It has four portals and was initially intended as a guest palace for royal visitors to the city. But the port below was too noisy for them.

FLY IN AMBER

Helen of Troy 14,000 years ago would have worn amber, that yellowish and brown, translucent and hard fossil resin the Polish call *bursztyn* and ancient Greek ladies knew as *Elektron* or Substance of the Sun, because wearing an amber necklace occasionally created tiny sparks. Some 50 million years ago the forests of the Baltic shore oozed tonnes of resin. The climate cooled, the forests were buried under ice, the climate warmed, the Baltic Sea was formed and the forests re-emerged – fossilized. The largest amber mine is near Kaliningrad, producing 90% of Baltic amber, while Gdańsk and Polish jewellers are the leading manufacturers. Jurassic Park-like insects have been preserved in amber and the trade earns Poland US$300m annually.

Down by the Riverside ★★★

At night a light beams down Długa (Long) Market from the Golden Gate to Green Gate, a pollution-measuring device. These gates were, of course, the medieval entrances into the fortified city. Green Gate is where **Lech Wałęsa**, hero of Solidarity and later President, has his office. The Dutch influence can be seen in the building. Blink one eye and you would think you were at Amsterdam's main railway station. It leads right onto **Green Bridge** across the Motława River with its cruise boats, yacht basin and **riverside walk**, or **Długie Pobrzeże**, of restaurants, jewellery shops, art galleries and old granaries on **Spichlerze Island**, opposite. There used to be 300 granaries in the halcyon days of the grain trade.

Strolling along the Motława and flanking the historic Main Town, you pass the 1450 **Bread Gate** or **Brama Chlebnicka** (there was a gate for every trade in the Middle Ages), then **St Mary's Gate** leading up into town and its magnificent church, followed by **Holy Spirit Gate** and then, most impressive of all, the massive **Gdańsk Crane** or **Żuraw Gdański**, the largest in medieval Europe. It was manpower-driven by treadmill and remained functional for 500 years. It was capable of lifting four tonnes. Floodlit at night, it is awesome and inevitably gazed at by tourist revellers on board a pirate sailing ship that plies the river. One of the granaries has been converted into the smart 281-room **Królewski Hotel** and yacht basin. The crane is part of the **Maritime** or **Morskie Museum**, with sections on both sides of the waterfront. The exhibits include the maritime history and trade of Gdańsk from the earliest Slav settlement. A ferry takes you across and you can actually walk round from Green Gate.

Below: *The Gdańsk Crane or Żuraw Gdański, the largest in medieval Europe, could lift loads of up to 2000kg. It is now part of the wharfside Maritime Museum.*

St Mary's Church ★★

The largest ancient brick church in the world, and the largest church in Poland, the **Kościół Mariacki** can fit 25,000 people. It was built over a period of 159 years starting in 1343. It has seven spires and three towers. In 1502, when this cavernous church was finished, the population of Gdańsk was only 30,000 (it is 461,000 now). Its interior covers an area of around 5,000m² (18,000 sq ft). It is 105m (345ft) long, has 37 gigantic windows, 31 chapels and 300 tombstones in the floor, and it is 405 steps up the 78m (256ft) bell tower to the viewing platform. The largest bell, 'Gratia Dei', weighs 7850kg (nearly 8 tonnes) and was cast in 1970. The 1470 **Astronomical Clock** at 14m (46ft) was the world's tallest clock at the time.

Above: *Construction in brick, such as St Mary's Church, was typical when Gdańsk was German-ruled.*
Opposite: *Soaring monument to the Solidarity martyrs near the now closed shipyards.*

The church's seven entrance doors include the **Shoemaker's Door** and the **Purse-maker's Door**. The crucifix in the **Chapel of the 11,000 Virgins** is Gothically ghoulish. According to a much-relished legend, its creator nailed his future son-in-law to a cross so as to get the agonized expression just right. **Hans Düringer**, the creator of the cross, apparently had his eyes put out so that he could never duplicate his masterpiece. Medieval Christianity's continuous depiction of sin and pain probably reflected the short and brutish lives of the time. Eulogistic and heavenly cherubs had to wait for the Baroque era. The church claims to have the largest stained-glass window in Poland. In Reformation days it became a Lutheran church and remained so from 1572–1945. The **Royal Chapel** is next door.

St Mary's Street, Ulica Mariacka, with its huge church is a fine example of close-packed, matched steps, verandas and houses, all rebuilt with gargoyle dragon gutters. These stone terraces were the focal point of social life in Gdańsk.

The Great Armoury ★★

The Great Armoury, in ornate Dutch Renaissance or Mannerism style, was completed in 1609. It is an impressive sight from both Targ Węglowy (Coal Market) and Piwna Beer streets.

The **Solidarity Monument** to the workers shot in the shipyard strikes of 1970 by the communist authorities is not far from the railway station in an open grassy roundel off Jana Z Kolna in front of the shipyard gates. It consists of three towering 42m (138ft) crosses of stainless steel from which at the top are suspended three brass anchors; all told, 140 tonnes. It was erected in three months, an incredibly short time, together with a poignant **Memorial Wall** commemorating those who died.

The **Grand Mill**, or **Wielki Młyn**, located in the street of the same name is 660 years old. Built by the Teutonic Knights on an island in the Radunia Canal, it may well have been the largest industrial plant of medieval Europe. Its 18 mill wheels, turned originally by slaves, ground away until 1945.

The small town of **Elbląg**, 60km (37m) south-east of Gdańsk, is a 10-minute drive from the 80km (50-mile) long **Wiślana Lagoon** – this was a perfect hideaway for Hitler's U-boat production in World War II with easy access to the open sea through the lagoon mouth of Baltijsk, now in Russian territory.

The sea-facing side of the lagoon is a long, forested sandbar with pristine beaches, sea birds and that unique Baltic wilderness. Poland's frontier with the Russian Federation lies halfway along it, at the gorgeous **Piaski** with its lovely sailing stretches.

Pomerania ★

Pomerania was first attacked by German-speaking warlords in about AD1000. Polish-speaking Slavs settled the Polish plains around the 8th century and by 990 King Mieszko I had united the Poles, converted to Christianity and put himself under the protection of both the German Emperor and the Pope. Some 230 years later, Poland, threatened by heathen Prussians (not Germans) and Lithuanians, invited the Teutonic Knights to help. But by 1308 these guests had turned on the Poles and captured Gdańsk (or Danzig). Although the Knights were eventually thrown out, German influence in Poland's Gdańsk remained strong until 1945, and Germans are still the largest tourist contingent.

The area to the west of Gdańsk is Pomerania, a German name associated with the USA's War of Independence. Its long coastline is holiday land. **Słupsk** and **Koszalin** are its two largest towns, with Ustka, Darłowo, Mielno and Kołobrzeg the main holiday resorts. Perhaps the best is **Kamień Pomorski**, which is home to the small but lovely part of the huge **Szczecin Lagoon** formed by the Odra River delta – **Woliński National Park**.

Stettin/Szczecin, the large Baltic port on the lagoon, is a town of 400,000 that has been Polish since 967. It was the native city of **Catherine the Great**, Empress of Russia, from 1762 to 1796.

Right: *Burghers' town-houses in Szczecin, brightly repainted in the Dutch style.*

Gdańsk and the North at a Glance

May–September are best for this seaside holiday town.

Good air connections from London, Warsaw and several German cities. The main train station (Dworzec PKP) is the decorative Gdańsk Główny station with the bus station (Dworjec PKS) opposite. There are ferries from Sweden.

Good bus, tram and tri-city train networks. Buy a book of 3 bus tickets at 1.40 PLN each on the bus. Taxis are not expensive by European standards.

LUXURY

Hanza, ul. Tokarska 6, tel: (058) 305 3427, www.hanza-hotel.com.pl 60 rooms in the Old Town. Ask for waterfront dockside-view room.

Zhong Hua (Sopot), ul. Wojska Polskiego 1, tel: (058) 550 2020, www.zhonghua.com.pl 49 rooms; bay views, Chinese decor, flowers and cuisine in Gdańsk.

MID-RANGE

Hotel Lival, ul. Młodzieży 10–12, tel: (058) 552 0200, www.hotel-lival.pl 35 rooms; new beachside establishment, tasteful decor.

Stara Karczma, ul. Stary Rynek Ollwski 7, tel: (058) 552 5159, www.starakarczma.com.pl 20 rooms in a restored inn, fresh flowers.

BUDGET

Abak (Mac-Tur), ul. Beethovena 8, tel: (058) 302 4170, www.abak.gda.pl Family-run pension, 12 rooms, ten minutes by taxi from railway station. Other pensions in the area, and a supermarket.

Wentur, ul. Drwęcka 7, tel: (058) 303 3001, www.wentur.gka.pl Quiet, suburban milieu. Satellite TV; nine rooms. Good value.

Polish and Kashubian Cuisine:

Mestwin, ul. Straganiarska 21–22, tel: (058) 301 7882. Seats 60. Mugs of beer to wash down hearty meals of potatoes, meat and cabbage. Open daily 11:00–22:00.

Myśliwska, ul. Jaśkowa Dolina 114, tel: (058) 341 7027. Seats 100. Hunting Lodge. Spit roast grill, goose, deer, wild boar. Open daily 11:00–22:00.

Palowa, ul. Dluga 47, tel: (058) 301 5532. Seats 500. Town Hall. Medieval banquets with duck, eel, pigs' trotters. Open daily 11:00–23:00.

Russian Cuisine:

Newska, ul. Grunwaldzka 99–101, tel: (058) 341 4646. Seats 120. Traditional heavy furniture, caviar, *pelmeni*, vodka. Open daily 10:00–22:00.

Lithuanian Cuisine:

Pod Lososiem, ul. Szeroka 52–54, tel: (058) 301 7652. Seats 120. Gdańsk's oldest. Chic antiques-loaded restaurant. Open daily 12:00–23:00.

Sea Cruises to Hel Peninsula, tel: (058) 301 4926. Żegluga Gdańska. www.zegluga.pl

Canal Cruises Elbląg to Ostroda, 80km, tel: (089) 646 3871, www.zegluga.com.pl

Malborg. Teutonic Knights' Castle. Daily train every 30min.

Słowinski National Park. Sand dunes, near coastal Leba, 150km (93 miles) by car.

Tourist Information Centre, ul. Heweliusza 27. tel: (058) 301 4355. Near main train station. Mon–Fri 09:00–16:00.

Online Information: www.gdansk.pl *Gdańsk in your Pocket* is an English-language listings guide (thrice yearly) available at newsstands, www.inyourpocket.com **Taxis:** Try Hallow, tel: (058) 9666.

Emergencies (when using a mobile phone): 112.

GDAŃSK	J	F	M	A	M	J	J	A	S	O	N	D
MAX TEMP °C	1	1	4	9	15	19	21	21	18	13	7	3
MIN TEMP °C	-3	-4	-1	2	7	11	14	14	11	7	2	-1
MAX TEMP °F	35	35	40	48	59	66	70	70	64	55	44	38
MIN TEMP °F	27	25	30	36	45	52	58	57	51	44	36	31
RAINFALL mm	33	31	27	36	42	71	84	75	59	61	29	46
RAINFALL in	1.3	1.2	1.1	1.4	1.7	2.8	3.3	3.0	2.3	2.4	1.1	1.8

4. Toruń and Poznań

Toruń is a fabulous old city straight out of a historical epic, an almost untouched fortified medieval trading town on the Vistula complete with Gothic spires, cobbled alleyways, bastion gateways, leaning towers, crenellated ramparts, Teutonic castles and monasteries. There's not a skyscraper in sight. It is also a university town and the birthplace of Mikołaj Kopernik (Nicolaus Copernicus), the famous astronomer. Naturally, it is also a Unesco site.

TORUŃ

Toruń consists of the Old Town (Stare Miasto) and the New Town (Nowe Miasto). In fact both are very old. Interlinked, they date back 800 years to the era of the Teutonic Knights and the river-borne grain-rich Hanseatic League, a union of trading cities in northern Europe. Toruń was the knights' first fortified base and launch pad from which to attack the 'pagan' Prussian tribes to the east.

If you would like to orientate yourself and save 'Old Toruń' centre for last, there is a variety of places of interest. A stroll across the **Wisła Bridge** (Bulwar Filadelfijski riverside promenade and onto Slimak Getyński sliproad) will give you a panoramic view across the waters to the Old Town, while at the opposite end of town to the river, once you have crossed the frantic Generała Sikorskiego road that marks the edge of the old city, is the quiet **Ethnographic Park**. The **Ethnographic Museum** (open daily) features both historical and contemporary life in northern Poland, plus a reconstructed traditional wooden rural buildings complex or *Skansen*. A green belt surrounds the city.

DON'T MISS

★★★ **Wisła Bridge:** panoramic view of the Old City of Toruń.
★★★ **Old Town, Toruń:** medieval architectural wonderland.
★★ **Copernicus's Statue:** outside the Old Town Hall (and Museum) in Toruń.
★★★ **Old Market Square (Poznań):** with its torture pole and drinking fountains.
★★★ **Town Hall (Poznań):** billy goat clock.
★ **Citadel Hill (Poznań):** park and outdoor Russian Military Museum.

Opposite: *The modern town centre of Toruń is a colourful meeting spot.*

Old Town Toruń ★★★

The Old Town was where the wealthy merchants lived. Starting at the Riverside Promenade you face a line of ancient fortifications, from **Sailor's Gate** with its three perfect arches – once the start of Toruń's Royal Walk – to the high Flanders-style **Convent Gate** named after an ancient Benedictine nunnery. Nearby, down a little alleyway, is the 15m (49ft) **Leaning Tower**, tilting 140cm (nearly 5ft) off the perpendicular and still standing after 600 years.

Copernicus's House is a typical Hanseatic merchant's house in Copernicus Street. It is also a museum. He was either born here or at No. 36 Old Market Square. Left into Żeglarska Street is the huge old **Market Square** dominated by the monumental bulk and tower of **Old Town Hall**, one of the largest medieval buildings in Europe.

Town Hall and Market Square ★★★

A statue of Toruń's most famous son, Copernicus, stands on a plinth fountain at the tower corner of the Old Town Hall which was built in the late 14th century by the Grand Master of the Teutonic Order, Conrad von Wallenrode, to signify Toruń's importance as a focal trading point of the Hansa trading conglomerate. The league always had its priorities right: the ground floor was for bread and cloth. The 40m (131ft) tower dates from 1274; its spire was destroyed during the Swedish siege of 1703. The hall is also the **Town Museum**. Check out the stained glass, a Toruń speciality, and climb the tower.

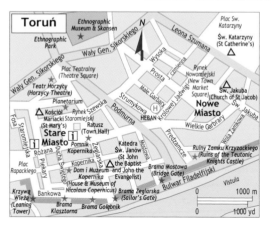

Hansa merchants built their houses to impress. Rows of them surround the town hall interspersed with large trees and many a pavement café and souvenir stall. The houses include **Meissner Palace**, the patrician **Schotdorff's Tenement**, the 1389 **Royal Pharmacy** (still operating) and the lavishly decorated golden five-storey **Star Residence** and **Museum of Oriental Art**. Tsar Peter the Great of Russia stayed here.

Gothic Cathedrals ★★

Christianity started 2000 years ago in what is today Israel and Palestine. It spread eastwards to India and south to Egypt, but its main thrust – due mainly to the evangelist Paul of Tarsus – was to the great Greco-Roman empires that ruled the western world.

Christianity came to Poland some 1100 years ago. One immediate result was the construction of huge Gothic cathedrals built to praise God, and demonstrate to non-Christians the power of the new religion and new rulers.

St Mary's Church (Kościoł Mariacki) just off the main square is a leviathan of red brick built by the Franciscan or mendicant Grey Friars as a monastery in 1239. In turn, it was Catholic, then Reformation Lutheran, then Catholic again. It is a mix of sombre Gothic and colourful Renaissance.

In similar red-brick Teutonic style is the **Katedra Św. Janów** or **Church of Saints John the Baptist and John the Evangelist**. After Kraków's Wawel it has the largest bell, 'Tuba Dei', in Poland. Starting in 1260, the church took 200 years to build.

The church's 'Digitus Dei' or 'Finger of God' clock has only one hand, which was normal at the time. The VIII numeral was unfortunately hit by a Swedish cannonball in 1703. The church, with its high stained-glass windows, contains the font where Copernicus was baptized and a startling 1478 mural of the devil, a cautionary tale.

POZNAŃ

Poznań is where modern Poland began even though Gneizno, 50km (31m) to the east, was the first capital. A fortified settlement on the island that divides the Warta River was in existence 1250 years ago. It was in Poznań in AD966 that Poland converted to Christianity and a cathedral was built on the first settlement, **Ostrów Tumski** or **Cathedral Island**. It soon became the capital of Wielkopolska or 'Greater Poland'. The Gothic cathedral on the

POZNAŃ'S CHURCHES

There are at least 16 churches in the old parts of Poznań, including the Franciscan Church, Adalbert's, St Martins, St Philip Neri, Bernadine, All Saints and St Margaret. The oldest church is on Cathedral Island. Then there is the pink and white Jesuit **Parish Church of St Stanisław**. He was the Bishop of Kraków (1072–79) who excommunicated King Bolesław II, was consequently murdered by the king and became the patron saint of Poland.

Below: One of the four massive ancient gates, or Brama, which lead past fortified walls into the Old Town.

island contains the tombs of the first kings of Poland and, reputedly, St Peter's sword. It was devastated in World War II and rebuilt.

Legend has it that three Slav brothers, Lech, Czech and Rus (note the countries), met after many years and the town they launched was named Pozna – 'to meet'. In fact the town's name derives from the personal given name Poznań. Today the city, on the west bank of the Warta River, is a centre of learning, scientific research and industry. However, its medieval heartland is well preserved.

Old Market Square ★★★

Stary Rynek, or **Old Market Square**, was demarcated in 1253 and it remains today the huge cobbled heart of old Poznań, focused on its lofty spired **Town Hall** in the centre. This is where the great and mighty built their four-storey gabled Baroque and Renaissance town homes, and this is where everything was noisily bought and sold, and still is. Today crowds stroll past façades, fountains (one at each corner) and cafés, and a replica of the torture pole

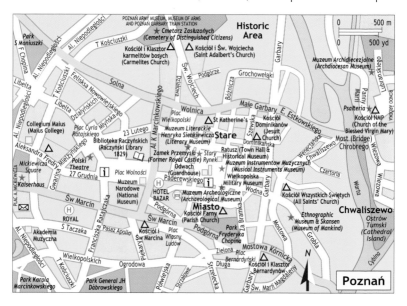

where criminals were dismem-
bered, a gory highlight of
medieval voyeurism. It was fin-
anced in 1535 by fining fancy
ladies who were dressed to kill.

Town Hall ★★

Begun in the late 13th century the
soaring spire – topped by
Poland's white eagle – of the
largely Renaissance Town Hall
dominates the huge square, each
side 140m (459ft) long. The
Gothic cellars below were completed in 1310. Someone with a
sense of humour later added a
pair of white billy goats to the

tower who, at noon, just above the town's clock, pop out
and ram each other 12 times as a bugler trumpets away.
The clock was known in 1551 as the 'ludicrous machine'.
The **Renaissance Room** and the multi-vaulted **Grand
Entrance Hall** house the delightful **Museum of the History
of Poland** (10th century to 1945).

Behind the **Merchants' Houses** is a lovely statue of a
peasant Bamber woman carrying pails of milk, commemorating the arrival in the 18th century in Poland of
German immigrants from the Bamberg area. The Town
Hall was destroyed by fire in 1536, but rebuilt.

Museums and Galleries ★★

There are 22 main museums and art galleries in Poznań.
Six of these are devoted to aspects of Poland's epic struggle
to retain and fight for its independence from invading
Swedes, Germans, Austro-Hungarians, Russians and its
own Soviet-imposed Communist government.

There are 40,000 items in the **Wielkopolska Military
Museum** in Old Market Square, while the **Poznań Army
Museum** documents the history of military science and
martial arts from the Uprising of 1918–19 to the forlorn
battles of 1939 against the invading Nazis.

Above: *The* Ratusz *or
Town Hall. Its size and
Moorish turrets dominate
the Old Marketplace.*

WE WERE THE FIRST

Step aside Warsaw, Kraków
and Poznań, for it was
Gniezno (pronounced
'Gneeyezh-no') that was the
first capital of Poland. Sitting
alongside a lake, 50km
(31 miles) east of Poznań,
the tiny town of Gniezno is on
the Piast Route highlighting
locations associated with
Poland's Piast or First Dynasty
that united the warring tribes
of the area under the white
eagle emblem of Poland.
Gniezno has a population
today of 73,000.

WHITE EAGLE

Gniezno, legend has it, was founded by the mythical character Lech, grandfather of the Piast Mieszko I (960–92). Out hunting on one occasion, as every Polish child well knows, Lech found a nest, or *gniazdo*, with a white eagle in it and it was thus he named the town and Poland's emblem. The eagle has always fascinated humans. Austria, Germany, Russia and the USA have all adopted the eagle as their national symbol.

Below: *Fountains and gardens create a quiet corner near the neo-Romanesque Kaiserhaus or Zamek Cultural Centre.*

Eighteen forts once surrounded Poznań. One, **Fort VII**, Colomb, the first Nazi death camp in Poland, includes a variety of heart-rending prisoners' possessions.

The **Museum of Arms** sits in an 1872 military bunker on Citadel Hill just outside the city. Its outdoor displays, in a lovely park, include Russian World War II tanks, and one of the first Katyusha rocket launchers, or Stalin Organs, mounted on a Studebaker truck. The **Museum of Poznań** documents the anti-communist struggles for bread and freedom of June 1956, 1968, 1970, 1976, 1980–81 and the triumphant final one of 1989. Some Poles collaborated with the invaders before and during World War II – a Europe-wide phenomenon – but Churchill once observed that Poland was the only country in Europe that never collaborated with the Nazis and no Polish unit ever fought with the German army.

Parks and Castles ★★

Sights of special interest in Poznań include the **Morasko Meteorite Nature Reserve** 8km (5 miles) north of the city centre. Its name is derived from seven round craters formed by falling meteorites 5000 years ago. The largest is 100m (328ft) across and 13m (43ft) deep.

The **Citadel Hill** makes a nice wooded walk. Apart from the display of Russian tanks, one cemetery includes the graves of Allied airmen killed in the 'Great Escape' from Sagan POW Camp in World War II.

The **Kaiser's Castle** is a huge neo-Romanesque stone edifice in Św Marcin Street, complementing two towering hawser-strapped crosses in **Mickiewicza Square**, a memorial to the Polish people's protests of 28 June 1956.

Toruń and Poznań at a Glance

Any time. April/May and September/October are ideal.

Toruń: Regular trains from Warsaw and Gdańsk. Hourly bus service from Warsaw. **Poznań:** Regular trains from Toruń and Kraków. Poznań is on the main Paris-Berlin-Warsaw-Moscow rail line.

Toruń is a 10-minute taxi ride from train or bus station to the Old City. Poznań's Główny train station is 2km southwest of the Old Town.

Toruń
LUXURY
Heban, ul. Małc Garbary 7, Toruń, tel: (056) 652 1555, www.hotel-heban.com.pl 30 rooms, central, historic.
MID-RANGE
Kopernik, ul. Wola Zamkowa 16, Toruń, tel: (056) 652 2573, www.kopernik.torun.pl 100 rooms, near the river and Old City. It is owned by the army.
BUDGET
Trzy Korony, Rynek Staromicejski 21, Toruń, tel: (056) 622 6031. 15 rooms. Superb location on main Stare Miasto Square. Ask for that view.

Poznań
LUXURY
Brovaria, Stary Rynek 73/74, Poznań, tel: (061) 858 6868, www.brovaria.pl 40 rooms. Main Square, perfect location.

MID-RANGE
Royal, ul. Św. Marcin 71, Poznań, tel: (061) 858 2300, www.hotel-royal.com.pl 40 rooms. Courtyard. Lobby has photos of almost-famous guests.
BUDGET
Dom Turysty, Stary Ryneck 91, Poznań, tel: (061) 852 8893, www.domturysty-hotel.com.pl 40 rooms in reconstructed 1798 Market Square residence.

Toruń
Petite Fleur (it's also a small hotel), ul. Pickary 25, tel: (056) 663 4000. Up-market Polish cuisine. Seats 40.
Zajazd Staropolski, ul. Żeglasrska 10–14, tel: (056) 622 6060. Seats 40. Polish food.
Pod Aniołem, Rynek Staromiejski. Vaulted cellar pub beneath the Town Hall. Cabaret, live music.

Poznań
Bażanciarnia, Stary Rynek 94, tel: (061) 855 3358. Excellent Polish cuisine. Seats 60. Overlooking Market Square.
Restauracja Stara Ratuszowa, Stary Ryneck 55, tel: (061) 851 5318. Polish food. Old vaulted cellar, antiques. Seats 60.

Restauracja u Garniewiczów, ul Wrocławsk 18, tel: (061) 853 0382. Polish, Lithuanian, Ukranian cuisine. Seats 60.

Toruń
Golub-Dobrzyń 14th-century Teutonic castle and museum. 40km (25 miles) east of Toruń.
Chełmno. Quaint rural town surrounded by medieval fortified walls. Bus from Toruń 51km (32 miles) north.

Poznań
International Knights Tournament in July. Jousting on horseback.
Wielkopolska National Park. Forest lakes, cycling and hiking trails, 25km (16 miles) south of Poznań.

Toruń: Tourist Information Centre, Rynek Staromiejski 25, tel: (056) 621 0931, www.it.torun.pl
Poznań: Tourist Information Centre (CIT), Stary Rynek 59/60, Market Square, tel: (061) 852 6156, 09:00–17:00 Mon–Fri, 10:00–14:00 Sat. Also: City Information Centre (CIM), tel: (061) 851 9645. Also at the airport.

POZNAŃ	J	F	M	A	M	J	J	A	S	O	N	D
MAX TEMP °C	1	1	7	12	20	23	24	23	19	13	6	3
MIN TEMP °C	-5	-5	-1	3	8	11	14	13	9	5	1	-2
MAX TEMP °F	33	34	44	54	67	72	76	73	67	56	43	37
MIN TEMP °F	24	22	30	37	47	52	57	55	48	41	33	28
RAINFALL mm	24	29	26	41	47	54	82	66	45	38	23	39
RAINFALL in	0.9	1.1	1.0	1.6	1.9	2.1	3.2	2.6	1.8	1.5	0.9	1.5

5
Warsaw

Warsaw reflects its terrifying recent past, when the very streets seemed to echo the agony of invasion, hate and destruction. The might of Hitler's Reich and Stalin's equally depraved Red Army, however, could not destroy the city's spirit. Pulverized street by street during World War II until it was an obliterated smoking ruin, it has risen from the ashes and is today once again a modern, vibrant, multicultural city of pizzazz, hi-tech industry, cuisine and home to 1.7 million people – the go-getting capital of Poland.

Warsaw, or in Polish Warszawa (pronounced 'Varshava'), had a settlement on the banks of the Vistula River going all the way back to the 10th century but it wasn't until 1413, roughly the era of Henry V in England, that **Janusz (the Elder)** made Warsaw the focal point of his **Duchy of Mazovia**. In 1596 **King Zygmunt III**, now united with Lithuania, moved the Polish capital to Warsaw from Kraków.

The 18th century saw Warsaw's peak, particularly in cultural life, but not for long; by 1795 Warsaw was forcibly incorporated into Prussia. At the 1814–15 Congress of Vienna that divided up Europe between those powers that had defeated Napoleon, Warsaw this time was integrated into Russian-dominated Poland.

As they had always done in the past, the people of Warsaw did not take it lying down. They rose up in 1830, only to be crushed. In 1914 the Germans occupied the city. It was returned to Poland in 1918, but was again devastated in World War II.

DON'T MISS

*** Palace of Culture and Science: Soviet-built King Kong skyscraper.
*** Royal Castle: 300 rooms filled with art.
*** Old Town Square: cobbled streets, flower sellers, cheesecake.
** New Town: as old as the Old Town; massive medieval walls.
* Wilanów: park and palace 6km (3.7 miles) from Warsaw.

Opposite: *Volunteers helped rebuild the 17th-century Royal Castle, deliberately destroyed by the German occupiers in World War II.*

Opposite: The Royal Castle looks out over Plac Zamkowy to St John's Cathedral and the Old Town.

Fury in the Ghetto

The Nazis forced the Jews of Warsaw into a ghetto – those they did not immediately force into their death camps. But to their astonishment (were not these *untermenschen*, these sub-humans, supposed to go like lambs to the slaughter?), the Jewish Poles fought back. In 1943 those left of the original 450,000 Jews in the ghetto, led by 1000 militants armed only with a few pistols, rifles, machine guns and home-made weapons, held off crack German troops, Lithuanian militia and, to Poland's subsequent shame, Polish police and fire-fighters, for 27 days of ferocious urban guerrilla warfare.

Eventually the Nazis set the ghetto on fire, street by street, and then used smoke bombs and flooded the sewers when the Jews tried using them to escape. Warsaw's 600-year-old Jewish community that formed the nucleus of Warsaw's intellectual, medical and cultural life was all but wiped out, 7000 shot immediately. There were only a handful left to surrender. This level of barbarity was equalled only by Poland's other neighbour, the Russians, who captured 8000 Polish officers in 1940 and at Katyń near Smolensk in Belarus machine-gunned them to death, an episode they tried to blame on the Nazis, but admitted their 'error' in 1990. The recently opened **Warsaw Uprising Museum** is a must.

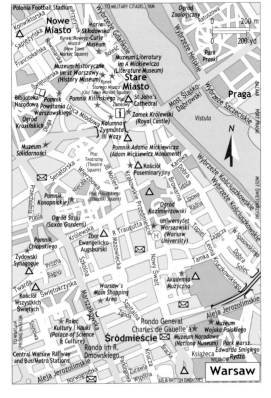

Hitler's Revenge

Hitler, of course, was furious that Jews had dared

rise up against him, a fury compounded when in August 1944 almost the whole population of Warsaw rose up under AK Commander Tadeusz Bór-Komorowski's home army of 400,000. For 63 days they fought the occupiers, and for the next three months Hitler's anger saw Warsaw destroyed. Women and children were lashed to tanks; 85% of Warsaw's buildings were destroyed and 850,000 (two thirds) of its population were killed or reported missing.

While all this was going on, Stalin's Red Army cynically sat on the other side of the Vistula River, content that Hitler was doing their intended destruction for them. So, on 17 January 1945, the Soviet Army 'liberated' Warsaw. There was, in fact, nothing to liberate. It was all in ruins. Only the women were left to rape, household goods to steal. The Poles (with a nod to the Hungarians) are the toughest and most determined of all Europeans. The people of Warsaw rebuilt their city in just 10 years.

Palace of Culture and Science ★★★

No matter where you are in Warsaw, one building is always visible, the so-called **Palace of Culture and Science**. It looks like New York's Empire State Building – with wings. Built by Stalin in 1952–55, it is a stone layered 'cake of abomination' 231m (7581ft) high and, in its grey sandstone Soviet Baroque, uglier than all of Stalin's many sins. Forty million bricks went into its construction, which covers an area of 3.32ha (8.2 acres) and has nearly 3300 rooms. This alien monster is either loved or hated in Poland. It has become a landmark, a real Warsaw icon near the railway station, and today has a bazaar – the

DEAR AND BELOVED RADIUM

Maria Skłodowska, also known by her married name, **Marie Curie**, was born the daughter of Polish teachers in Warsaw, then under Russian partition, in 1867. At the age of 24 – women being forbidden by the Russians to go to university – she left for Paris and the Sorbonne where eventually she became Professor of Physics and the first woman to teach at the Sorbonne. She and her husband discovered two new radioactive chemical elements – polonium (after her mother country) and radium – and jointly won the Nobel prize for Physics in 1903. In 1911 she won her second Nobel prize, this time for chemistry, for isolating pure radium. Due to prolonged exposure to her 'dear radium' she died of leukaemia.

Above: *Palace of Culture and Science. This 'King Kong' confection, gift of the Soviet Union, dominates Warsaw's skyline.*

Rozycki Bazar – in the Plac Defilad in front of it. There is a viewing deck from the top floor, as well as a concert hall, cinema and café. Yes, it is the devil's wedding cake (rock climbers love it). One walks around it, stupefied by its bulk, height and appalling ugliness. You have to see it. You – literally – can't miss it.

The Old Town ★★★

The Old Town, on the banks of the Vistula River between the Śląsko-Dąbrowski and Gdańsk bridges, was completely and miraculously rebuilt as a 17th- and 18th-century town utilizing every tiny piece of original masonry not totally destroyed by Hitler. Even the cobblestones had to be replaced. It is small by the standards of other old towns in Poland, but replete with sights – neo-historical buildings, hackney cabs, buskers, flower sellers and fleece-the-tourists action. This also is Warsaw, and a welcome relief from the austere cling-wrap condo architecture of the new city and its wide sidewalks and hurtling traffic.

Royal Castle ★★★

The entry point into the Old Town is the Baroque **Zamek Królewski** or **Royal Castle**. You can tell you are getting near by the sound of wild folk and pop music from the open-air stage next to it in Plac Zamkowy. The castle's origins go back to the 14th century and it has been the seat of Mazovian dukes, Polish kings, Russian tsars (lots of onion bulb spires) and Polish presidents. It was blown up in the war but reconstructed between 1971 and 1984. It has in its 300 rooms a storehouse of art, including those of the grandiose huge-canvas 19th-century Polish master **Jan**

Matejko, so loved by all Poles. The **Royal Apartments** are exquisite, rebuilt and decorated – ironically – according to archival records from the equally devastated German city of Dresden. The **Canaletto Room**'s 23 paintings – cityscapes – document Warsaw as it was in the mid-18th century, and hence were invaluable in the rebuilding of Warsaw's historical monuments. The sumptuous **Royal Chapel** has a funeral urn enclosing the heart of **Tadeusz Kościuszko**, Poland's 18th-century revolutionary military hero who was awarded honorary citizenship of both France and the USA. Cutting out hearts was a Spanish custom much used by the Austrian Habsburg emperors, and very fashionable at the time.

The **Marble Room** and **Ballroom** are exquisite. In the latter, in 1806, Napoleon made his legendary compliment – much quoted in Poland – about the sublime beauty of Polish women.

Old Town Square ★★★

Little winding cobbled streets, boutiques festooned with adverts and gleaming amber windows constitute Warsaw's visitor hub. **St John's Gothic Cathedral** is the oldest church in Warsaw. The Nobel prize-winning author of *Quo Vadis*, **Henryk Sienkiewicz** (1905), is buried here. The square – surrounded by a handsome mix of Gothic, Baroque and

Left: *All the buildings behind this carriage in Old Town Square were completely rebuilt after World War II.*

Renaissance buildings, with its sun umbrellas, old drinking fountain, Kantor money-changers, *dorozki* (horse-drawn carts), quick-pix, buskers playing didgeridoos, artists, little old ladies selling posies of flowers, dozens of cafés and a thousand milling visitors – is something out of Chaucer's *Canterbury Tales*. And to think that, other than two tank-blasted walls, tenements, No. 34 and No. 36, it was all a wasteland of rubble and smoking ruins in 1945.

The **Historical Museum of Warsaw** runs the length of the northern flank of the square (the entrance named after an old Inn sign *Pod Murzynkiem* – Under the Black Man – at No. 42). It has 60 rooms on three floors. Check the documentary (in English at midday) about the wartime levelling of the square and its reconstruction.

In the western corner of the square, along the narrow ul. Nowomiejska with its summertime artists and the occasional old flame-torch holder stuck into a wall, you come to the Barbakan, gate, fortress, parapet, ramparts and massive semicircular walls that guarded the medieval town. There are grand views of the Vistula below.

Below: *Barbakan towers guard the Nowomiejska Gate between the Old and New towns.*

New Town ★★

The new town or **Nowe Miasto** is not new at all. It was built in the 14th century, a few years after its 'old town'

cousin adjacent to it. It was the home of 'the people' rather than the aristocracy. Ul. Freta 16 was the family home and is now the museum of **Maria Skłodowska (Marie Curie)**, double world prize-winner in physics and chemistry in the early 20th century.

The New Town's square consists of reconstructed 18th-century houses. The **Church of the Holy Sacrament (Kościół Sak-ramentek)** was built by

Polish King Jan Sobieski's wife Maria to commemorate his decisive victory over the Ottoman Turks at the siege of Vienna in 1683.

Park Łazienkowski ★★

The **Royal Way**, as it is called, leads from the **Royal Castle** for 4km (2.5m) to **Łazienki Palace** (the name actually means 'baths') and its lovely park, one of a dozen parks in and around Warsaw, all of which give a welcome green lift to this city of concrete and memory.

Łazienki Park was once the royal hunting preserve – a favourite pastime of royals, then and now – surrounding **Ujazdówski Castle** and was snapped up by King Stanisław Poniatowski in the 1760s for him to turn it into one of the fashionable French-style parks, with avenues of oaks, lake, open-air summer concerts, the **Chopin monument**, **Old Orangery** and the elegant neoclassical Italian-designed **Palace on the Water**, or **Pałac na Wodzie**, on an island over a stretch of lake using the existing 100-year-old bathhouse, hence the name, 'baths'.

The palace is now a museum of fine art and arty collectibles. There is a **Botanical Garden**, **Museum of Hunting and Housemanship**, some ferocious animal frescoes in the **Biały Dom (White House)** where Stanisław housed his mistress of the day, an **Observatory**, and the usual pubs and cafés.

Wilanów ★★

Another Park 'n' Palace complex, 6km (4 miles) south of Łazienkowski, Wilanów (pronounced 'Villanoof') was the summer residence of the fighting **King Sobieski** who, in Renaissance mood, called the property Villa Nova, hence its name today. It is the most splendid of Warsaw's many palaces and set in exquisite high rural surroundings on the edge of the city. The palace is almost Versailles-like in its grandeur, its impeccable gardens and its wide open spaces. The palace itself can only be visited by advance-booked guided tour. It is not cheap, but worth the money.

The palace was developed by King Jan III Sobieski, who was not exactly what one would call modest. The **Grand**

RIVER OF TRADE

The Vistula or Wisła River, rising in the southern Carpathian mountains that divide Poland from Slovakia, flows gently through Kraków, Warsaw and Toruń to enter the Baltic Sea 1090km (677 miles) later near Gdańsk. It basically divides Poland into east and west and has been the conduit of trade between northern and central Europe since before Roman times. Seven bridges cross the Vistula in Warsaw where it is some 300m (985ft) wide.

BIZARRE BAZAAR

Warsaw's main city sports stadium is called Dziesięciolecia near the Poniatowskiego Bridge on the Praga side of the Vistula. Initially known as the Russian Market, it is Europe's largest outdoor market with nearly 3500 stalls. You will hear accents from all over Europe and the world. Jugglers, water tumbler musicians, pop singers and immovable statue ghosts entertain. A tray of switchblades, second-hand leather coats, smuggled Marlboros, fast food, Rayban shades from Beijing, the occasional 'guaranteed' icon, designer toiletries, kitchen appliances, rosaries – everything is on sale. In many ways it is a vast version of an old medieval market square. Turnover daily is in millions. Unfortunately it is due to be 'cleaned up' before the Euro 2012 Football Championships.

Above: *Turkish war spoils helped King Sobieski build Wilanów Palace.*

TO THE WOODS

The **Kampinos Forest National Park**, or **Puszcza Kampinoska**, stretches west from Warsaw in a 45km (28-mile) arc back from the Vistula River and covers an area roughly the size of Greater Warsaw. It is mainly oak, birch and pine forest, daunting and beautiful in its winter coat when the spoor of large flat-antlered elk, beaver, fox, lynx and more rarely tusked boar can be seen in the pristine snow; boar is a favourite on Polish menus. There are 300km (186 miles) of hiking trails in the park. Beware of swamps, climb the 30m (100ft) forested dunes and don't get lost.

Entrance Hall, two storeys high, sets the tone. There are some 60 rooms, lots of wonderful furniture, *objets chinois*, porcelain, silver vases, works of art (those not taken by the Nazis) and a museum. The **Great Crimson Room** is a must. It drips with *décor riche* and Latin quotes from Virgil. Sobieski is usually seen mounted on a horse and vanquishing Turks.

The gardens include a **Chinese summerhouse** (china and ceramics), an **Italian Baroque Garden**, a **Poster Museum**, a **church**, a **guardhouse**, the **Orangery** with temporary art exhibitions and a section of the park described wistfully as the 'Romantic English-Chinese Park'.

Katyń Museum is 2km (1.25 miles) from Wilanów. Opened in 1993, it shows memorabilia and details of how 8000 Polish officers were abducted by the Red Army in 1940 and executed for fear they would be the core of any resistance to Stalin.

The few remains of a notorious Nazi death camp, **Treblinka**, are only 80km (50 miles) northeast of Warsaw. Some 800,000 Jews were murdered here in 1942–43. Bodies were burned at a rate of 5000–17,000 daily. The whole area has been re-forested.

Warsaw at a Glance

May–September are best. Warsaw can be bitterly cold in winter with a freezing wind.

Many airlines operate to Frédéric Chopin or Okęcie Airport (flight information tel: (022) 650 42 20, www.lotnisco-chopin.pl). Bus No. 175 takes you to the old town via Warszawa Centralna (the main train station). The main bus station, Warszawa Zachodnia, is 3km (2 miles) west of the centre.

Bus, train and Metro. The latter is only one line. For all transport timetable information, tel: (022) 9484, www.ztm.waw.pl Tickets for all three from newspaper or tobacco kiosks where you see the MZK decal, and on board. One-day, three-day, and one-week passes are available. Plenty of taxis, try Radio Taxi, tel: (022) 9621.

Warsaw is similar in price to weathier European cities.

LUXURY
Le Meridien Bristol, ul. Krakowskie Przedmieście 42–44, tel: (022) 551 1000, www.warsaw.lemeridien.com 250 rooms, famous 160-year-old restored hotel. Originally owned by Ignacy Paderewski.
Le Regina, ul. Kościelna 12, tel: (022) 531 6000, www.leregina.com 60 tastefully decorated rooms in a new smallish hotel. Courtyard.

MID-RANGE
Harenda, Trakt Królewski, ul. Krakowskie Przedmieście 4–6, tel: (022) 826 0071, www.hotelharenda.com.pl 150 rooms, second night free at weekends.
Ibis, Stare Miasto, ul. Muranowska 2, tel: (022) 310 1000, www.ibishotel.com Popular with businessmen, 150 rooms.

BUDGET
Mazowiecki, ul. Mazowiecka 10, tel: (022) 827 2365, www.mazowiecki.com.pl 60 rooms (15 en suite), central.
Zajazd Napoleoński, ul. Płowiecka 83, tel: (022) 815 3068, www.napoleon.waw.pl 40 rooms; Napoleon's choice on his march to Moscow.

Bar Pod Barbakanem, ul. Mostowa 27–29. Cheap commuters' diner. *Pierogi* and *jurek* soup. Seats 60. Open daily 09:00–17:00.
Restauracja Dom Polski, ul. Francusca 11, tel: (022) 616 2432. Seats 100. Elegant terrace-garden dining. Open daily 11:00–23:00.
Dekerta, 38–42 Old Town Square, tel: (022) 635 6511. Seats 80. Old Polish cuisine.

Kolomyja, 23 Od Lasu Str, Konstancin-Jeziorna, tel: (022) 754 0594. Seats 200. Wagon wheels, smokehouse. Open daily 11:00–23:00.
Memora, 2 Plac Grzybowski, tel: (022) 620 3754. Seats 120. Jewish cuisine, Israeli wines. Open daily 11:00–23:00.
U Fukiera, 27 Rynek Starego Miasta tel: (022) 831 58 08. Old Town Square. Sidewalk café. Seats 150. Serves the best cheesecake in Poland.

City Tours: Mazurkas Travel, tel: (022) 629 1878.
Biking and birding: Kampio, tel: (022) 823 7070.

Warsaw Tourist Information (City Tourist office), tel: (022) 94 31, 474 11 42, www.warsawtour.pl
Classical Concert, Opera and Theatre tickets: Kasy ZASP, Mon–Fri 11:00–18:30, tel: (022) 621 94 54.
Police/Ambulance/Fire: From a mobile: 112
Hospital Emergencies, LIM Medical Centre, Al. Jerozolimskie 65/79, tel: (022) 458 70 00, www.cmlim.pl/en

WARSAW	J	F	M	A	M	J	J	A	S	O	N	D
MAX TEMP °C	0	0	6	12	20	23	24	23	19	13	6	2
MIN TEMP °C	-6	-6	-2	3	9	12	15	14	10	5	1	-3
MAX TEMP °F	32	32	42	53	67	73	75	73	66	55	42	35
MIN TEMP °F	22	21	28	37	48	54	58	56	49	41	33	28
RAINFALL mm	27	32	27	37	46	69	96	65	43	38	31	44
RAINFALL in	1.1	1.3	1.1	1.5	1.8	2.7	3.8	2.6	1.7	1.5	1.2	1.7

6
The Lake District

The northeast of Poland has always been a cross-current of peoples and cultures: Poles, Russians, Belarusians, Tatars, Jews, Teutonic Knights and Lithuanians. The borders have continuously shifted and moved with wars, invasion, religion and politics. There are over 2000 lakes and rivers in the area stretching from the present Lithuanian border 58km (36 miles) north of Suwałki, and vast forests, swamps, national parks and peat bog wilderness. Not many visitors come here, even Poles. But it is a peaceful and extraordinarily beautiful land centred on the towns of **Suwałki**, **Augustów**, **Olecko** (known as Treuburg in German times), **Ełk**, **Giżycko**, **Kętrzyn** (Hitler had his vast command bunker here during the 1941 invasion of Russia), then the lovely Lakeland resort village of **Mikołajki** and historical **Olsztyn** in the west. The East Prussian border used to run within 20km (12 miles) of Suwałki and German is still understood in the area. There is also a Lithuanian minority nearer the eastern border, as many as 40,000 people.

Suwałki ★

You would probably not write home about the little (population 68,000) town of Suwałki. It is largely a transit point on the way to the beautiful surrounding lakes and forests. But the **cemetery** – divided up into Catholic, Jewish, Lutheran, Orthodox, Old Believer and Muslim Tatar sections – gives an idea of its once volatile mix of cultures. The Suwałki area is the spiritual home of Nobel prize-winner **Czesław Miłosz**.

Don't Miss

★★★ Lake Wigry Monastery: Pope John Paul II stayed here and so can you.
★★ Walk in the Forest: you can also fish in Lake Wigry.
★★★ Mikołajki: lakeside resort village with sailing, exploring, lovely restaurants.
★★ Mazurski Park: Łuknajno Wild Swan Reserve has 2000 swans in this wilderness 4km (2.5 miles) from Mikołajki.
★★ Olsztyn Town: entry point for Mazurian Lakes.
★★ Castle at Olsztyn: Copernicus the astronomer lived here for three years.

Opposite: *Lake Wigry's church; the monastery itself is now a hotel.*

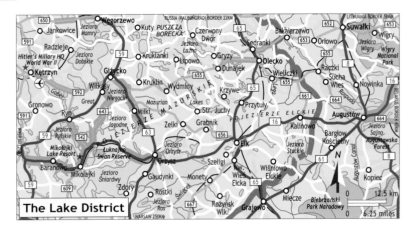

The Lake District

You may come across the **Orthodox Old Believers**, or **Starowiercy**, with their 'molenna' places of worship, in this area (one in Suwałki). Some of them still live in old wooden houses eschewing such modern decadences as tea, coffee, alcohol and tobacco. The town was actually founded by the Camaldolite monks in 1715, from their beautiful **Wigry Monastery** on an island in the nearby lake.

The beaver is a large, humped, amphibious rodent with a broad flat tail, webbed hind feet and soft brown fur, much sought after in the 19th century for tall President Lincoln-type hats. The beaver is the symbol of **Wigierski National Park**. It covers an area of 15,085ha (37,275 acres) and is a 15-minute drive from Suwałki.

Apart from the forests of spruce-pine, oak and birch there are 1000 species of plant, 200 moss species and 300 kinds of lichen. Mammals in the park include elk, roe deer, boar, badger, wolf and fox. There are 180 species of bird including the white-tailed eagle and the lesser spotted eagle. In its 73m (240ft) deep lake waters there are 32 species of fish. The **Czarna Hańcza** canoe route (which starts north of Suwałki) passes through **Lake Wigry**. The park is ideal for hiking (with 130km/80 miles of trails), horseback riding and cycling. The **European Through-Hiker-Route-E.11** from Amsterdam runs through the park. Some 50 small farmers in the park offer B&B accommodation.

Wigry Monastery ★★★

By the end of the 18th century, the Wigry Monastery prop-
erties covered 300km² (116 sq miles) of land, forest, lakes,
56 villages, 11 granges and Suwałki town. The **Wigranie**, a
'pagan' Yotwingian tribe ethnically and linguistically similar to Lithuania and old Prussia, survived the bloody
Teutonic conversion invasions and settled on Lake Wigry
island. Then came the Lithuanians. In 1418 the Grand
Duke of Lithuania and Polish King Jagieło (Władysław V) –
who had defeated the Teutonic Knights at the cataclysmic
battle of Grunwald – came hunting here, as did King
Zygmund II August, in the next century. Between 1648
and 1652 King Jan II Kazimierz (John Casimir) built a hunting lodge here, and then in 1667 handed the lodge and
island over to the **Camoldolese Order** who over the next
50 years built the monastery. They introduced highly
skilled land husbandry, forest and water projects, brick-
yards, a papermill and glassworks. The monks themselves
lived in isolated hermitages, now visitor lodges.

Although devastated by war on many occasions and
now no longer a monastery (the order was dissolved by
the Prussians), the buildings and church were continuously
restored. Today the church is still well attended and its
lodges, cellar restaurant and rooms surrounded by the fish-
rich lake and forest attract many a visitor, including a
variety of country fairs, folk-dancing gatherings, fishermen
and, in June 1999, Pope John Paul II, who chose Wigry as
a break from his Polish pilgrimage. It's easy to see why:
rural beauty, isolation, peace and tranquillity. The area is,
however, snowbound for four months a year.

Great Forests ★★★

The **Augustów Puszcza**, a primeval forest, covers an area
of around 1100km² (425 sq miles), and is Poland's second
largest area of forest. Named after King Zygmund August
in 1557, it consists mainly of pine and spruce with sections of hornbeam, oak, elm, lime, maple, birch and aspen
all contributing to a dappled panorama of light and dark
as the sun plays in the trees or off the reeds that fringe the
numerous waterways.

DEVIL FISH OF WIGRY

Barnabus, a young friar-cook
in the Camaldolese monastery,
anxious to please his prior,
promised to get him a white-
fish or lavaret for supper, his
long-time favourite. But such
fish were only available in
Italy. So he sold his soul to the
devil. The appropriate
Faustian document was
signed, and the devil flew off
to get the fish. Barnabus, fear-
ful of what he had done,
confessed all to the prior. By
this time the devil, fish in his
claws, was approaching Lake
Wigry. When the prior rang for
matins earlier than normal, the
devil took fright, knowing the
young monk had reneged on
his pledge, and angrily threw
the fish into the lake. Since
that time, visitors to Wigry
monastery have been able to
enjoy this delicious fish.

BISON OF BIAŁOWIEŻA

The European bison was almost wiped out. By 1916 there were only 150 remaining in the Białowieża forest, the last and largest sweep of primeval lowland forest left in Europe. Today, thanks to a breeding programme and security in the **Białowieża National Park**, there are not only 300 bison there but 3000 worldwide. The European bison (*żubr* in Polish) weighs in at 1000kg (2205 lb) and can charge at 50km (30 miles) an hour. Although not as viciously cantankerous as the African buffalo, don't take any chances with a bison.

The whole forest extends for 1260km² (487sq miles). It lies 75km (47 miles) from the industrial town of Białystok where Ludwig Zamenhof (1859–1917) invented the Esperanto language.

For park tours, cycling and walking trails, call the PTTK office, tel: (085) 681 2295.

Wolves, wild boar, beaver and elk are in the forest, but have sufficient wilderness savvy seldom to be seen. Bird life includes cranes and grey herons. The **Augustów Canal** is a 102km (63-mile) waterway through the forest linking the Biebrza and Niemen rivers. It was built 170 years ago to provide Poland with an alternative to the Vistula outlet to the Baltic. It has 18 locks, with many a boat excursion available from Augustów in summer.

Białystok (pronounced 'Byoweestok') has a population of 280,000 and developed as a textile manufacturing town in the 19th century. Half its population (particularly its Jews) was slaughtered by the Nazis in World War II.

The **Knyszyńska forest** is right on the eastern border of the town and it stretches south to join the **Białowieża National Park**, a Unesco World National Heritage Site that not only has bison but also oak trees that are over 300 years old. For more information about the park, visit www.pttk.bialowieza.pl/eng.htm

The 17th-century **Orthodox Monastery of St Basil** can be seen in the forest at the village of Supraśl. This whole area is both Catholic and Orthodox with an admixture of Tatar, descendants of the 13th-century Mongolian invasion that swept southeastern Poland.

Mazurian Lakes **

Lake Śniardwy, Poland's largest lake, stretches 20km (12 miles) east and south of the charming little (population 4000) lakeside resort village of **Mikołajki** (pronounced 'Meekowhykee') halfway between Suwałki and Olsztyn and right in the middle of Mazuria's lake district, which in turn is fringed by the towns of **Mrągowo** (American country music), **Święta Lipka** (320-year-old original four-towered late Baroque church), **Kętrzyn** (Hitler's Wolf's Lair bunker complex), **Węgorzewo** (northernmost reach of the Mazurian lake system) and **Giżycko**, a post World War II rebuilt holiday resort. The village of Mikołajki out of season is a delight, with its plastic 'king of the white fish' fountain, square, yachts, sailing boats, lake bridges, waterside promenades, tourist fish and chips, Lutheran church (and museum), some excellent restaurants and nearby

White Swan Reserve. It calls itself the Mazurian Venice, which it isn't, but it does have architectural integrity and a certain medieval-village style.

Stately Sailing Swans

Mazurski Park surrounds the shallow 700ha (1730-acre) **Łuknajno Swan Reserve** lake 4km (2.5 miles) east of Mikołajki. It is possibly Europe's largest remaining reserve of *Cygnus olor*, the mute white swan.

Mazurski Park is a Unesco biosphere sanctuary wetland harbouring 175 bird species of which 95 nest here. A long wooden deck leads to the reeded water's edge where a high platform enables you to see the swan-clouded lake, especially in July and August when the beautiful creatures moult their feathers, or in April and May when they nest. Central Europe and Central Asia are the swan's natural homeland. They feed by immersing head and neck up to a metre in the water, feeding on aquatic plants, frogs, worms and insects. Both parents tend their half a dozen young for up to five months. The species has been introduced into many other countries.

Olsztyn ★★

It would be easy to dismiss Olsztyn (pronounced 'Olshtin'), an industrial town with a population of

Left: *Everyone, it seems, goes down to the lake in boats at Mikołajki.*

170,000, as merely a rebuilt entry point to the Mazurian lakes. It was actually burnt to the ground in typical Nazi-Soviet style in 1945. However, just off the busy Piłsudskiego intersection there is a lovely riverside walk and park below the castle walls that leads to the rebuilt 14th-century **Castle**, **Museum** and **Old Town**. In the middle ages, Olsztyn was the southernmost bastion of the Teutonic Knights, then was ceded back to Poland a century later. After the first Partition of Poland between Russia and Prussia, a habit Hitler and Stalin emulated, it formed part of East Prussia until 1945 when all Germans were ethnically cleansed.

Copernicus's Town

Olsztyn lies in Warmia between the provinces of Pomerania and Mazuria and is named after the Warmians who, like other local tribes, were wiped out by the Teutonic Knights in a fit of religious excess. The area has always been a tug-of-war between Prussians and Poles and was only finally returned to Poland after World War II.

The **High Gate**, the Gothic **Brama Wysoka**, is all that remains of the medieval battlements. It leads to the **Rynek** or **Market Square**. These market squares in medieval times were the equivalent of our modern shopping centres: they offered food, entertainment, trade, music, socializing, town hall, places of worship (cinemas today) and the occasional well-attended execution. The town's skyline is festooned with peaks, coronets and fancy façades built according to the century, taste, historical fashion and wealth of the individual merchant.

The **Castle**, compact and almost impervious to attack, was where **Copernicus**, the famous Polish astronomer, lived for three years. In fact, he was the Warmia administrator from 1516 to 1520.

Below: *Olsztyn's Brama Wysoka or High Gate.*

The Lake District at a Glance

May–September are best.

By train from Kraków via Warsaw to Suwałki in the east or from Olsztyn in the west. There are also long-distance buses.

Your own or a hire car is best for off-the-beaten-track lakes.

MID-RANGE
Wigry Monastery (Wigry Lake near Suwałki), Dom Pracy Twórczej w Wigrach, 16-412 Stary Folwark, tel: (087) 563 7000 or 563 7019. It has 25 rooms and chalets. When there are no conferences this superb monastery is budget cheap.
Hotel 'Na Skarpje' Mikołajki, ul. Kajki 96, tel: (087) 421 9950, or 421 6418, www. hotel-naskarpie.pl It has 30 rooms; overlooks lake.
Pensjonat Mikołajki, ul Kajki 18, Mikołajki, tel: (087) 421 6437. Eight rooms in a three-storey 'family' wooden house on the lakeside promenade.
Folwark 'Łuknajno' (Lake Łuknajno Wild Swan Reserve near Mikołajki), Łuknajno 2, tel: (087) 421 6862 or (087) 421 6437, e-mail: folwark@mazury.info Ten rooms in an old farmhouse on the lake. Splendid isolation.
Hotel Pod Zamkien (Olsztyn), ul. Nowowiejskiego 10, Olsztyn, tel: (089) 535 1287, www.hotel-olsztyn.com.pl

There are 18 rooms in this private hotel (rather like an Elizabethan hunting lodge) below the castle walls.

Suwałki
Dom Nauczyciela, tel: (087) 566 6900. Seats 80. Best restaurant (hotel) in this small passing-through town.

Lake Wigry
Dom Pracy, tel: (087) 563 7019; details the same as for Wigry Monastery (*see* Where to Stay). Charming monks' refectory-restaurant in the monastery cellar. Open until 21:00. Seats 100.

Mikołajki
Bella, Plac Hanlowy 11, Mikołajki, tel: (087) 421 5247. Seats 30 inside, 50 on the summer patio. Superb fish dishes in this elegant little restaurant. (Rooms available). Recommended.
There are a couple of other good restaurants on this same square. On the 'High Street' and lakeside promenade there are several cafés, waffle or *gofry* outlets, fish stalls, pizza spots and other fast-food joints catering for summer sailing fans.

Olsztyn
This old provincial town has a population of 170,000 but no legacy of cuisine. Meals are *pierogi* wholesome and cheap at pubs and cafés. Try:
Villa Pallas, ul. Żatnierska 4,

tel (089) 535 01 15. Hotel restaurant. Seats 60. 60–80zł.

Canoeing Trips Ten days on the Czarna Hańcza River and lakes, starting point usually the village of Augustów 31km (19 miles) south of Suwałki. Lakeshore hostels; bring wellies and sleeping bag. Contact PTTK in Augustów, ul. Nadrzeczna 70A, tel: (087) 644 3850, or PTTK in Olsztyn, ul. Staromiejska, tel: (089) 527 5156.
Lake Boat Trips Open deck steamers (with snack bars), 2–7 hours. Operated by Żegluga Mazurska. Buy tickets at passenger jetties. Routes include the interconnecting lakes of Mikołajki. Giżycko, Ruciane and Węgorzewo. You can also sail off in a high-masted pirate-like sailing ship at Mikołajki. This village is a favourite with both Polish and German budget groups.

Suwałki Tourist Office, ul. Kościuszki 45, tel: (087) 566 5494, www.suwalki-turystyka.info.pl
Forma-t Tourist Bureau, ul. Noniewicza 93, loc 10A, Suwałki.
Mikołajki Tourist Office, plac Wolności (main square). Open May–Sept 09:00–17:00, tel: (087) 421 9062, www.mikolajki.pl
Olsztyn Tourist Office, plac. Wolności (near the high entrance gate), tel: (089) 535 3565.

7
Lublin and the East

Lublin is one of the oldest human settlements in Poland dating back to within 100 years of the fall of Imperial Rome in AD500. In the 9th century, during the times of Charlemagne, there was a sizeable trading colony here on the banks of the Vistula. In the 12th century, era of the Crusades, a defensive stronghold was built where the castle stands today. In 1569 the so-called **Lublin Union** united Poland and Lithuania, creating the largest European state at that time, stretching from the Baltic to the Black Sea. A century of trade and prosperity followed. Then it was partitioned and fought over by the Habsburg Empire, Russians and Swedes. After World War I, a Catholic university was established here, the only one in Eastern Europe. It flourished right through the communist era.

Lublin is today an important industrial centre, a development that fortunately has not affected its magnificent historical centre.

Streets of Lublin

Lublin's main street is the **Krakowskie Przedmieście**. Its wide, restaurant-lined reach stretches past a bronze billy-goat fountain, street violin buskers, the 15th-century **Church of the Holy Spirit** built in the Lublin Renaissance style and the **New Town Hall** to the **Brama Krakowska**, or Kraków Gate, the old main gate (closed at night), one of three into the old town. The **Historical Museum of the City of Lublin** is housed here. You have to cross the busy circular **Lubartowska Street** to get to its great vaulted arch topped by a Baroque spire, a favourite with street artists,

DON'T MISS

★★★ **Krakowskie Przedmieście Street:** take a leisurely stroll down to the Old Town.
★★★ **Old Town Hall:** from 1389; Merchant Princes Palaces.
★★★ **Great Castle:** like a Crusader fort; market.
★★★ **Castle Chapel:** exquisite Slav Byzantine frescoes.
★★ **Old Churches:** 15 major churches.

Opposite: *Lublin's neo-Gothic crusader castle shines white in the sun; its frescoed chapel is stunning.*

curio hawkers and old ladies selling tiny posies of flowers. Krakowskie runs into Bramowa Street, the start of the Old Town proper. Little cobbled medieval streets (Dickensian at night) twist off this main throughway that eventually heads to the **Castle**.

Market Square ★★

The much rebuilt 1389 **Old Town Hall** sits plumb in the middle of a huge square – an oversized cream-coloured neoclassical clump. It practically squeezes everything else out as the elegant four-storey multicoloured merchant princes' palaces enclosing it seem to fight for space. These were built in a variety of eclectic styles reflecting the multinational composition of Lublin: Armenian, Greek, Scottish, Russian. There were also Lublin mayors from countries such as Italy, France and Germany. Gothic, Renaissance, Baroque and other styles are all represented. No. 17 reveals a plaque indicating that in 1835 Polish violinist, **Henryk Wieniawski**, was born here. (His father played safe and converted to Christianity.) The **Crown Tribunal on the History of the City** is in the Old Town Hall, while No. 12, **Konopnicka House**, is where Charles XII of Sweden and Peter the Great of Russia were once guests. The square is a good place to sip a coffee and watch the constant two-way flow of children's educational groups, chimney sweeps, dog walkers and late-for-an-appointment business people. The ochre-coloured house at the northeast corner, No. 8, was the house of the 16th-century **Lubomieski family**. Its restaurant has some entertainingly explicit 14th-century frescoes in its three-storey wine cellars, including one of the oldest representations of Lublin town. It was the seat of the **Jewish Kehillah** and is now an art gallery.

Below: *Pedestrians enjoy strolling down Krakowskie Przedmieście in Lublin.*

Old Churches ★★

On the horseshoe circular peri-
phery of the old town are several
massive churches, some 15 in
Lublin. On Ul. Krówleska, the
Dominican Church and Monastery
was founded in the 14th century
and reconstructed in the 17th with
somewhat doubtful Baroque additions. Then comes the **Cathedral**,
with its spires and columns, built in
1586–1625 for the Jesuit Order.
The 'whispering acoustic' sacristy
has frescoes colourfully depicting
the 'triumph of faith over heresy'.

Above: *The 500-year-old Dominican church and monastery is huge.*

Another **Jesuit Church** is next on the same traffic-hurrying
street, and behind it the **Church of the Conversion of St
Paul**. The only functioning Protestant Church in the area is
the **Holy Trinity Evangelical Church** with its unique
tinned-plate coffin epitaphs.

There is also the rather magnificent **Transfiguration
Orthodox Church**, with its richly ornamental and
Baroque-like gold-plated iconostasis (a tiered screen that
separates sanctuary and nave) from the 1630s.

Old Jewish Lublin ★★

Medieval Catholics were raised to believe that it was 'the
Jews' who killed Jesus, forgetting that Jesus was a Jew
himself, thus the beginnings of anti-Semitism. Jews were
blamed for the plague, for fires, floods, invasion, and
even accused of killing children for satanic purposes. The
trouble was this was an age of ignorance. Jews had to live
apart, out of the city, in ghettos, could not be part of the
civil service and in fact were usually restricted to banking
(and trade, by special permission), since good Catholics
were theoretically not allowed usury – to make a profit.
The Jews were not only different in language, dress and
religion, they were also made to be different – stig-
matized. Anti-Semitism soon locked deeply into the
European psyche.

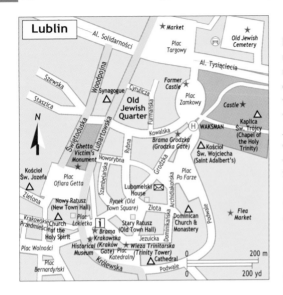

Attitudes in Lublin, however, were more relaxed and Jewish landmarks are worth tracking down. A **Talmudic Yeshiva** was allowed to be founded, while in **Podzamcze** a Jewish settlement developed on the northern slope of Castle Hill. In **Grodzka St**, a little way before the Grodzka Gate to the Castle, at the continuation of Bramowa No. 11, a plaque states: 'In the years 1862–1942 this building included the **Jewish Orphanage Ochronka**. On the 24th day of March 1942 the Nazis murdered all the children of our House'.

Grodzka Gate is also known as the **Jewish Gate**, because of the Jewish part of Podzamcze suburb stretching beyond it. It used to have a drawbridge 200 years ago. The gate area was used by Jewish shopkeepers. A museum here houses **Grodzka Gate Theatre** with a permanent multimedia exhibition on Lublin as it was in 1939. There is also a Jewish restaurant here, Szeroka 28.

Lublin Castle ★★★

The Old Town of Lublin is linked by a high drawbridge-like pathway to the heights of Lublin Castle, possibly because it was a marshy stream at one stage. In the 12th century Lublin became the seat of a 'Castellan', or 'Governor of the Castle', whose job it was to build a stronghold to protect his section of the turbulent frontier against raiding parties of Tatars, Lithuanians and Ruthenians from Ukraine. The Castle itself was begun by **King Kazimierz II (The Just)**. It was he who united Poland. Initially an earthen and wood fort was constructed and, in the 13th century, a heavily fortified brick Romanesque keep tower.

During this era of Dürer, Chaucer and Breughel, agricultural expansion led to huge population growth and hence to the rise of towns. It was a time marking the start of a uniquely European institution – universities – as well as water delivery, windmills, iron-casting techniques and soaring medieval cathedrals. The spinning wheel (and hence cheaper clothes) and soap were invented and gunpowder came into play. The Cult of Saints (saints were usually of 'noble family') and that of Mary developed. The Mongols in 1241 gave everyone a fright.

Lublin's old castle tower is still there today, dominating the huge Crusader-like fort. In 1569 the Act of Union with Lithuania – Poland and Lithuania have always had a love-hate relationship – was signed, the occasion immortalized in a patriotically romantic canvas by 19th-century Polish painter **Jan Matejko** who specialized in huge historically heroic works. This highly imaginative one, in the castle, is 5m (17ft) long and half as high.

The castle was destroyed in the mid-17th century but in the early 1800s was rebuilt in what was called English neo-Gothic (four square and crenellated Crusader battlements). It was a prison until 1954, but is now a museum with permanent exhibitions of Polish porcelain, silver, furniture and clocks, coins, folk costumes and military history, plus **Polish and European Art** of the last 400 years. The museum has four smaller branches in Lublin: **History of the City**, **Literature**, the **Manor House Branch**, and **Martyrology 'Under the Clock'**.

RENAISSANCE GEM

The Renaissance saw a grand flowering of thought, art, music and architecture, no more so than in the perfectly preserved 400-year-old town of Zamość 89km (55 miles) southeast of Lublin. Named after Jan Zamoyski, the enlightened chancellor of the town, Zamość has over 100 buildings, churches, monuments, grand merchant houses, a square, columned arcades, colourful façades and a magnificent Town Hall, all enclosed within powerful star-shaped fortifications, moats and lakes which kept its people safe from Cossacks and Swedes. Even the Nazis spared this beautiful town.

Left: *Lublin's grand white Castle dominates the town.*

Castle Tower ★★

The castle has been a Tsarist, Nazi and Soviet prison. Some 300 prisoners were killed here by the Nazis on 22 July 1944 before they abandoned Lublin to the Russians and communists in Poland, who in turn were responsible for 333 deaths in 1944–54.

No castle is complete without a deep and dark dungeon to incarcerate dangerous desperados. Lublin's **Castle Keep Tower**, a massive Romanesque-Norman defensive-residential structure, goes back 750 years.

It was erected on the south slope of a hill descending to a water ravine (now a grassy park leading to a huge market). It is circular, built of brick and limestone, has three storeys, walls of 3.4m (11ft) thick, and it stands 20m (66ft) high. An internal spiral staircase leads to the top with its panoramic views of Lublin.

Chapel of Beauty ★★★

The tower and **Chapel of the Holy Trinity** are the only remains of the original castle. The magnificent blue and gold two-storey Gothic vault of the chapel is supported by a single giant octagonal pillar in the middle of the square nave. The whole chapel, with its cross-ribbed vaulting, is covered with exquisite medieval Slavic-Byzantine frescoes of saints, prophets, angels and biblical scenes. **King Władysław Jagieło** had a Russian mother and she obviously influenced his taste in cosmic Church art. Painted by Ruthenian artists from the Ukraine, it represents the only instance where eastern artists here decorated a western Gothic church. Each panel story was completed in a single day. The *Passion of Christ* is particularly moving. And there is a pair of frescoes of King Jagieło, the missionary prince. The whole thing was completed on 10 August 1418 and signed as such by master artist Andrew. Incredibly, it was not discovered until 1897, having been plastered over. Restoration took 100 years, and was finally completed with the help of an EU grant.

The chapel is closed for ten minutes each hour to ensure ventilation, and it is air-conditioned to a continuous preservative temperature. Only 25 visitors are allowed in at a time.

Lublin and the East at a Glance

May to September, but there are good music and theatre festivals in Nov and Dec.

Lublin has no airport. If it did, it might well attract the number of visitors that Kraków does. There are good and fast train connections from Warsaw (175km; 109 miles) and less frequently from Kraków, a distance of 345km (214 miles) via Warsaw.

Both buses and trams are convenient. Taxis are relatively cheap. But you will do a lot of walking on the lovely cobbled alleyways of this old city. Taxi Service for the disabled, tel: (081) 533 3310.

LUXURY
Grand Hotel Lublinianka, ul. Krakowskie Przedmieście 56, tel: (081) 446 6333, www.lublinianka.com 72 rooms. Recently renovated pearls and polo pile. Weekend discounts.

MID-RANGE
Hotel Europa, ul. Krakowskie Przedmieście 29, tel: (081) 535 0303, www.hoteleuropa.pl 75 rooms, Holiday Inn-like hotel. (Always negotiate in Polish hotels especially Jul–Aug in cities and weekends.)
Campanile, ul. lubomelska 14, tel: (081) 531 8400, www.campanile.com.pl

French chain, very comfortable, 75 rooms.
Hotel Victoria, ul Narutowicza 58–60, tel: (081) 532 7011, www.hotel.victoria.lublin.pl Central, 60 rooms.

BUDGET
Waksman (Old Town), ul. Grodzka 19, tel: (081) 532 5454, www.waksman.pl Six rooms. Excellent choice.
Hotel Polonia, ul. Pogodna 36, tel: (081) 710 5470, www.hotel-polonia.pl 35 rooms.

Tamara Café, ul. Krakowskie Przednieście 36. Cul de Sac, underground vaulted cellar, fabulous decor and Chilean wine by the glass. Seats 60.
Bel Etage, ul. Krakowskie Przednieście 56, tel: (081) 446 6100. Grand hotel, olde worlde. Rooftop café in summer. Seats 80, more in café.
Piwnica Pod Fortuna, Rynek 8, tel: (081) 534 0304. Market Square. Elegant Polish cuisine. Seats 70.
Szeroka 28, ul. Grodzka 21, tel: (081) 534 6109. Seats 70. Jewish restaurant, live music.
Chata Swojskie Jadło, ul. Nadbystrzcka 16, tel: (081) 538

2525. Folk Music. Seats 65.
Hades, ul. Reowiaków 12, tel: (081) 532 8761. Seats 120. Popular, jazz and disco.

Underground Tunnels, Old Town tour. Wednesdays 10:30 from ul. Rynek 1, Crown Tribunal, tel: (081) 532 5867.
Marie Curie, Skłodowska University Botanical Garden, ul. Sławinkowska 3, tel: (081) 537 5543.
There are river bathing beaches, tennis clubs, bowling, flying, horse riding and rock climbing walls in Lublin.

Ambulance: 999.
Police: 997.
Central Coach Station, PKP Information: (081) 94 36.
Central Coach Station, PKS Information: (081) 747 6649.
Car Hire: (081) 743 3005.
PTTK Tourist Office: Rynek 8, tel: (081) 532 3758.
English-speaking guides: (081) 444 0900.
Tourist Information Centre (Old Town, Cracow Gate): ul. Jezvicka 1/3, tel: (081) 532 4412, www.loit.lublin.pl

LUBLIN	J	F	M	A	M	J	J	A	S	O	N	D
MAX TEMP °C	0	1	6	13	19	23	24	23	19	14	6	3
MIN TEMP °C	-7	-6	-2	3	8	12	14	13	9	5	1	-2
MAX TEMP °F	32	34	43	55	67	73	75	73	67	57	43	38
MIN TEMP °F	20	21	29	37	46	53	57	55	48	40	33	28
RAINFALL mm	27	24	25	43	57	88	105	93	58	50	43	43
RAINFALL in	1.1	0.9	1.0	1.7	2.2	3.5	4.1	3.7	2.3	2.0	1.7	1.7

8
Tatra Mountains

The snow-peaked Tatra (or Tatry) Mountains are gorgeous. The highest range of the Central Carpathians, they extend for 64km (40 miles) along Poland's southern border with Slovakia. The two countries cooperate closely in tourism. Mount Gerlachovka, or High Tatra, is the highest peak at 2655m (8710ft) and is actually just over the Slovak border. The Tatras are Poland's winter playground with 50 ski lifts, solitary beautiful lakes, sheep's cheese, wild flowers, forests, unique log cabin architecture, tumbling streams, husky dog competitions and enough local folklore, music and local cuisine in Zakopane – the main village – to tempt all visitors. In fact, three million visitors come to the Tatras each year.

Mountain Music

The foothills of the Tatra mountains stretch south of the 13th-century (uninspiring) farming town of Nowy Targ, or New Market, north of Zakopane, in a border arc from Lake Orava in the west to Lake Czorsztyn in the east, forming the Podhale area. It is these foothills of old wooden villages, cattle meadows, strip fields, roadside shrines and meandering valleys that are home to the Górale mountain people. They are a particularly proud, hospitable and no-nonsense people who have strenuously held onto their traditions of wood houses, highly colourful dress, dialect, customs and above all their fiendishly fast fiddle music, which has been adopted throughout Poland.

DON'T MISS

★★★ **Cable car to Mount Kasprowy:** mountains, forests and snowy peaks.
★★★ **Morskie Oko Lake:** glacial, mountain-hugged lake; flowers.
★★ **Walk in the mountains:** dozens of trails.
★★ **Zakopane music:** hear the frenzied violins.
★ **Zakopane shopping:** embroidered blouses and waistcoats.

Opposite: *Rafting on the Dunajec River dates back to 19th-century river logging days.*

The Tatra mountain region was 'discovered' by Polish writers and poets in the late 19th century and has flourished ever since. Zakopane is the main centre.

The Tatra area includes the mountainous **Górce National Park** and, in the east, the 1000m (3280ft) high **Pieniny Park** with its canoeing and leisurely 'whitewater' log pontoon rafting in the fast-flowing Dunajec River Gorge.

Festive Frenzied Zakopane

Snowmobiles, conferences, minibus hire, music, skiing lessons, barbecues, music clubs, pubs, mud riding, horse riding, parachuting, hang-gliding, water shooting, wildflower spotting (no picking, please), ski lifting, tramcar riding, day tripping, cave exploring, hiking, biking, drinking, eating, adventure climbing, tobogganing, snowman making, heated swimming, lake visiting, sleigh riding, spas, an aqua park, cross country skiing, cultural events, theatre, husky dog competitions, hackney cabs, folk dancing – the list goes on and it's all available in Zakopane, Poland's festive summer and winter playground.

Zakopane is 400 years old, originally a settlement of shepherds and farmers with only one water mill to its name. In the mid-18th century a steelworks was built in nearby Kuźnice to exploit Tatra iron ore and soon Zakopane was 'discovered'.

A hundred years later the town had become known all over Poland as a health spa and tourist resort. A parish was set up in 1845, the first hotel, Pod Giewontem, came in 1885, and four years later the railway arrived.

ATHLETIC POPE

Karol Wojtyła, or Pope John Paul II, was born in Wadowice in the foothills of the Tatra mountains 46km (29 miles) from Kraków. He was a writer, poet, actor, manual worker (breaking stones) and athlete. He loved walking in the clean air of the Tatra mountains and was a keen skier. He particularly liked the beautiful Chocho-łowska Valley which he revisited as Pope in 1982 and again in 1997.

Practically anything touched or visited by John Paul is revered in Poland. A 23-tonne monument has been made from Tatra mountain stone in his memory and when he died in 2005 a million Poles attended a thanksgiving mass.

Zakopane ★★

The **Chicha Woda River** flows through Zakopane to become the **Zakopianka**. It is joined by a dozen rushing streams from the surrounding mountains which all but envelop the town and the beautiful farming valley in which it is set. From south to north the town is only about 2km (1.25 miles) long (with the action confined to half its length) and a permanent population of 30,000. The main street – lined with boutiques, steak joints, faux-folkloric wooden restaurants, leaning street lights, billiard saloons and pubs – is called Krupówki; it is snowy and packed with visitors in the winter, even more in the summer. A little Japanese bridge crosses the **Potok Bystry** stream. Down near the circular market, past the new parish church, the noise of rushing water tinkles everywhere. Turn right and you come to the **Gubałówka** cable car station. The old cemetery sits on a hill behind. Its wooden **Church of St Clement** is where revolutionary Zakopane architect Stanisław Witkiewicz is buried together with his multi-talented son Witkacy and skier Helena Marusarzówna who was executed by the Nazis in World War II for her role in the Polish Resistance (AK). Most of Zakopane's houses (usually with big gardens) are in traditional peaked two- to three-storey wood, giving the whole town an impression of being a small village.

Wherever you are in Zakopane, look up and you will see mountains. They are so near, so omniambient, it seems you can touch them.

At the Pass

Just off Krupówski Street – almost everything is just off Krupówski Street in Zakopane – is the **Muzeum Tatrzanskie** (open 09:00–15:30, closed on Sundays, as are most places in Zakopane). This pretty little museum features the local Górale folk culture so well preserved in this area. There are a series of recreated wooden interiors of mountain and peasant farmer cottages and, of course, the colourful local costumes still worn at weddings and on special occasions: women in puffed sleeves, bodices

Above: *Cars give way to family farm carts in the cobbled market streets of Zakopane.*

and full flowing skirts, men in tight black-embroidered woollen trousers, cummerbands, decorated waistcoats and huge black feather-floating hats. Note the strapped pump-shoes. The costumes and customs of the Zakopone area are not unlike those of Slovakia across the border. Most of the Tatras are, in fact, in the latter country.

Zakopane may look crowded and touristy at times but it started out as very much a high society holiday refuge. The composer **Karol Szymanowski** (1882–1937), second only to Chopin, came here, mixing indigenous folk rhythm and excitement into his evocative music. He was one of a group of intellectuals who liked to think of themselves in the 1920s as the flag-bearers of vanishing Tatra culture. His ballet, *Harnasie*, his piano mazurkas and his highly popular song series *Seopiewnie* all come from the soul of Tatra. **Stanisław Witkiewicz** also did much to focus attention on local Podhale culture with his *At the Pass (Na Przetęczy)* book of 1891. The illuminati of Zakopane have included **Ignacy Paderewski** and **Henryk Sienkiewicz** as well as Karol Szymanowski. The Wiłkacy theatre in Zakopane is known throughout Poland.

Near the **Old Cemetery**, not far from the mountain vehicular station, is the **Villa Koliba**, Witkiewicz's first recreated mountain chalet. It is now the **Museum of the Zakopane Style**, and features Witkiewicz Senior's bulky wooden furniture plus some rather weird portraits by his son (*see panel, page 119*).

Gubałówka ★★★

Gubałówka is a long mountain ridge stretched out at a height of 1123m (3683ft). On one side it is a long slope of sheep farms and hamlets but on the high mountain facing side, it drops sharply to the long Zakopane valley and village with an almost endless 180° panorama of pine-forest and snow-capped mountains rising sharply above it end to end. Take a return trip on the tiered and glass-enclosed funicular, and come back (on the same ticket) on a four-person ski-chair which leaves from the far end of the ridge. From the top it is rather like being on a vast view platform – there's a vista of green, white and yellow and the blue of the crisp cold sky. The scene is stunningly beautiful.

A gravel road runs the length of the 2km (1.25-mile) ridge. It is crowded initially with wooden view platforms – and cuddling couples, ski lifts, eateries and souvenir shops – but off-season it is a lovely walk, with mountains on your left, sloping meadows on your right. You can walk up to Gubałówka if you prefer, and there is a bus service up the mountain connecting villages on both sides. The forested Gubałówka Ridge is the starting point for many a bracing mountain and forest hike, ending in such villages as Chochołów or Witów with their rustic wooden houses. There's a tiny chapel on top of Gubałówka and, of course, a children's adventure school among the pines. It is ideal for ski touring.

Mountains of the Sun

There are 26 peaks in the Zakopane Tatra range. It is their visibility, not height, that makes the Tatras so dramatic. Divided into three groups (and you can pan the length of them with your camera on top of Gubałówka), they rise from **Nosal** at a mere 1206m (3956ft) to the highest, **Lodowy**, at 2627 (8617ft). The nearest, seemingly about 5km (3 miles) away and in front of you, is the **Tatry Zachodnie Group** with the great snowy obelisk of Glewont phalanxed by the Długi Glewont ridge.

Mount Kasprowy Wierch ★★

Kasprowy Wierch, at 1985m (6511ft), is right on the border between Poland and Slovakia. Slovakia was part of Hungary for 900 years until 1918 when, together with Bohemia and Moravia, it became

---

FATHER AND SON

We all yearn for rural simplicity. Słanisław Witkiewicz (1851–1915), painter and art critic, came along with the perfect answer. He evolved the primitivist wooden Zakopane style of buildings – steep, pointy roofs for the snow and attic windows – using huge logs of pine and interlinked joints.

His son was equally talented. Słanisław Ignacy Witkiewicz (1885–1939), or Witkacy, was educated at home by his father. As a young man he was quite the lover, fought against the Russians in World War I and took to hallucinogenic drugs. Witkacy became an accomplished painter, photographer, philosopher, dramatist (sex and murder to the fore) and novelist. To demonstrate 'catastrophism' he committed suicide, thus guaranteeing his place in Poland's pantheon of unusual artists.

GLACIAL LAKE

You can take a horse-drawn cart the last 9km (5.6 miles) of the ascent to Morskie Oko (or 'Eye of the Sea') Lake, at altitude 1399m (4589ft). This lovely expanse (but crowded in April–August) of icy water is surrounded by alpine evergreen forest and meadows of purple, red and yellow mountain flowers peeking through the tough tufted grass. The soaring granite cliff faces rise sheer to the sun. It is, in fact, one of Poland's top visitor destinations. You can actually go by road and bus. A stone walking path circles the lake as it shimmers emerald then blue in the morning light, with the occasional raptor riding the thermals to swoop down near the reedy shore. There are at least 10 major alpine lakes in the Tatras.

Czechoslovakia. Slovakia became independent in 1993. It has a population of some 5.3 million people.

The cable car that takes you up from Kuźnice near Zakopane to the summit was opened in 1935, a route of 4290m (2.6 miles) taking 20 minutes. The views are stunning as you hover over forest and peak, sunlit gorges and swirling mist. The walk back – if you like – takes about two hours through the Gąsienicowa alpine pastureland or, for the more adventurous (rock climbers), west to the summit of Giewont, 'the Sleeping Giant', with its huge cross looking down on Zakopane. The downhill route is via the idyllic Kondratowa valley, a day's excursion

Dunajec Gorge ★★★

The 35km (22-mile) long **Pieniny** mountain range lies some 50km (31 miles) as the crow flies to the east of the Tatras. Like the Tatras, it is a national park. There are old wooden churches and a mountain castle in the little village of Niedzica, and superb hiking trails. The highest peak at 982m (3221ft) is the **Three Crowns**, or **Trzy Korony**, overlooking the twisting, roaring **Dunajec River Gorge** which rushes its way through 8km (5 miles) of soaring limestone rockfaces and jagged peaks. It is a canoeist's paradise with fast-swirling rapids that visitors have, for over 170 years, braved in large pontoon rafts lashed with ropes and steered by standing and amazingly dexterous oarsmen in the traditional blue and purple Pieniny Górale highland costume of leather cummerbunds and decorated half-jackets.

Right: *Skiers on the sunlit heights of Mount Kasprowy Wierch on the Slovakian border.*

The Tatra Mountains at a Glance

Any time of year. Spring and summer for mountain rambling. Skiing in winter (until early May).

Three hours by inexpensive Szwagropol bus leaving Kraków from Dworzec PKS bus station. Rail is another option (four hours).

The village is small enough to walk to any hotel, bus station, restaurant, or the cable car PKL train station to the Gubałówka Ridge. There are many ski-lifts.

LUXURY

Villa Marilor, Kościuszki 18, tel: (018) 200 0670, www.hotelmarilor.com It has 30 stylish rooms.

Belvedere, Droga do Białego 3, tel: (018) 202 1200, www.belvederehotel.pl Spa & gym, 35 classy rooms, just 1.5km from town.

Redyk, Zàb 48e Kało Zako-panego, tel: (018) 200 1661, www.redyk.pl 22 rooms in Zakopane architecture.

MID-RANGE

Sabaa, ul. Krupówki 11, tel: (018) 201 5092, www.sabala.zakopane pl 20 rooms and wood-furnished suites.

BUDGET

Dom Turysty, ul. Zaruskiego 5, tel: (018) 206 3207, www.domturysty.z-ne.pl

70 rooms, cheap en suites.

Pensjonat U Kośle, Podhalańska 51, tel: (018) 201 9222, www.ukosle.z-ne.pl 19 rooms, meals inclusive. Near ski-lifts.

Staro Jzba, ul Krupówki 28, tel: (018) 201 3391. Seats 40. Wooden alcoves, cottage and farm implements, cosy fire, icon-decorated walls. Live violin music. Recommended.

Karczma Regionalna Anna Gut, ul. Krupski 11, tel: (018) 201 5093. Seats 200. Vast glass-fronted log cabin with monster fireplace.

In **Zakopane visitorland** are bakeries (*Cukiernia Samanta*), a pizzeria and at least a dozen restaurants featuring deer, boar, fish, local Podhale Goralski foods including sheep cheese *oscypki*, pickled cabbage, mulled wine *bombolki* with honey and 'highland electric tea'. There's feverish (and delightful) folk music, dishes served by colourfully skirted almost-country girls. Nearly all the eateries are in the main Krupówki strolling street, and all similarly priced.

Skiing. Five areas. Best is **Kasprowy Wierch** at 1985m (6511ft). Ski pass length, 9700m (6 miles). Cable car from Kuźnice, short bus ride from Zakopane, then the chairlift. **Nosal Mountain complex**. Chairlift, length 650m (711yd). Lighting system and

partly artificially snowed.

Gubałówka. Just above Zakopane. Cable tram for 120 people at a time. Ski pass length 1600m (1750yd). Also artificially snowed slope with lighting. Ski school.

Mountain Biking. There are 650km of cycle routes. Plenty of rental options.

Tobogganing. Gubałówka slope, 750m (820 yds).

Hiking. Buy the English version of the Tatrzański Park Narodowy map (1:30,000) showing colour-coded paths. Beware of sudden cloud close-down. Do not go higher than treeline. Overnight huts available. Also beware of the 500kg, 2.8m tall brown bears.

Rock Climbing. By permit from Park offices, Chałubińskiego 44, tel: (018) 206 3799.

Fun for Children. Adventure Park Linowy on Gubałowka Ridge. Also Aqua Park Tatralandia, horse riding, holiday village. Whitewater river rafting (Pieniny mountains). Zakopane is particularly popular with Russians.

Ambulance: 999 or (018) 201 2082.

Mountain Rescue: (018) 206 3444 or 0-603 100 100.

Tourist Information Centre: Kościuszki 17, tel: (018) 201 2211.

Weather Information: tel: (018) 206 3019.

Mountain Guides: Chałubińskiego St 44, tel: (018) 206 3799.

Travel Tips

Tourist Information

Małopolskie Centrum Informacji Turystycznej, Cloth Hall Main Market Square. tel: (012) 421 7706 or 421 3051, www. polandtour.org
UK Tourist Office, Level 3, Westgate House, West Gate, London W5 1YY, tel: 08700 675 010, www.visitpoland.org
Judaica Cultural Centre, ul. Meiselsa 17, tel: (012) 430 6449, www.judaica.pl
The website of the official **Warsaw Tourist Bureau** is www.warsawtour.pl
Most towns have a **tourist office**. Look for the IT logo.

Entry Requirements

A passport is required, valid for at least six months after your date of departure. British citizens can stay for six months without a visa, EU and US citizens for 90 days. South African, Australian and New Zealand visitors should contact their nearest Polish embassy as visas cannot be obtained at port of entry.

Getting There

See page 62.

Health

There are no special health requirements or inoculations for entry into Poland unless you are coming from endemic disease areas (usually developing world countries – check online or with your travel agent). Immunization against flu is always a good idea (aircraft are notorious).

Public medical care in Poland can be a little erratic and staff are poorly paid. At times you may have to pay upfront to get attention and if hospitalized will have to arrange for friends to bring you meals. EU citizens are entitled to free emergency care, but in an emergency it is advisable to contact a 24-hour private health care clinic.

Polish tap water is perfectly safe in some places but not recommended everywhere, particularly in Warsaw. Most visitors drink water in the ubiquitous blue bottles. You are unlikely to eat tainted food in a society that enjoys going out for meals. If you get travel diarrhoea, the nearest – and inevitably efficient – pharmacy *(apteka)* will advise you to drink diluted Coca-cola and eat as little as possible until it clears up. Always travel with medical insurance cover just in case. Pharmacies require a doctor's prescription but if you can produce your original prescription details or even a few remaining pills there should be no problem in getting a repeat. Pharmacy staff usually speak some German or English.

There is HIV in Poland as in all countries. Contraceptives were once difficult to obtain in this Catholic country but are now widely available.

What to Pack

Poland is hot in summer and exceptionally cold in winter especially along the wide streets of Warsaw. Carry a small umbrella. Ties and jackets are seldom needed. Long trousers are normally worn in the evening. A pair of light binoculars is useful especially for the snowy Tatra Mountains in the south and the lake district in the north. Churches seem happy with shorts but they are not common except on the Baltic beaches in the summer. Put a Swiss army knife in your hold luggage for outings, and also a couple of novels as you will not be able to buy books in English except in the larger city stores. You can buy most other things locally. Poland can be very sunny in summer so sun cream, shades and hat would not be out of place.

Money Matters

The **złoty**, abbreviated to **zł** and pronounced 'zwo-te', is the unit of currency in Poland. (It means 'golden'.) It is divided into 100 **grosz**, or **gr**. The letters PLN are often written in front of an amount of złoty (e.g. PLN 250) to indicate Polish currency. The bank notes, each adorned with the head of a Polish king, are available in denominations of 10, 20, 50, 100 and 200 złoty. There are nine coins, ascending in value to 5zł. You cannot walk down a street in the cities especially Kraków without passing numerous foreign exchange bureaux, known as *kantor* in Polish. There are also plenty of banks and ATMs for all the main credit cards. The latter are regularly used in hotels, restaurants, car rental companies and the larger shops but less so in the smaller

Useful Phrases

A phrase book is not all that useful unless you are good at languages. You are quite likely to get out of your depth, and using a slick rehearsed phrase may land you with a torrent of unintelligible Polish in reply – although your embarrassment will break the ice! Rather carry a small Polish dictionary with you, such as Globetrotter's *Polish in Your Pocket*. With this you will be able to identify individual words, such as items you want to buy.

Here are a few of the most basic words you will need, with the approximate pronunciation in brackets:

Yes • *Tak* (tahk)
No • *Nie* (neh)
Please • *Proszę* (prosheh)
Thank you • *Dziękuję* (djehn kooyeh)
Good morning • *Dzien dobry* (djehn dohbri)
Goodbye • *Dowidzenia* (do veedzehnah)
Where? • *Gdzie?* (gdzheh)
When? • *Kiedy?* (kyeh-deh)
How much? • *Ile?* (eeleh)
One • *Jeden* (yehdehn)
Two • *Dwa* (dvah)

Here are some of the Polish words you are likely to see on signs:
Główny • Main (as in main market, main square)
Miasto • Town
Kościół • Church
Plac • Square
Ulica (ul.) • Street

establishments and country areas. Poland is not as plastic-oriented as e.g. Western Europe and the USA. Quite a few establishments will quote in euros, as there are many German visitors, and Poland will no doubt join that currency union eventually. The złoty has hardened of late and purchases are not as inexpensive as one might expect. At time of writing the złoty is worth roughly 4.5 to the pound, half that to the dollar and 3.3 to the euro. There is not much of a parallel or black market in currency. You can get very inexpensive meals if you are careful; cheap fast food from corner vendors and public transport is usually very good value. Traveller's cheques are not nearly as convenient as ATM credit cards.

Customs

Arriving in EU countries is always a pleasure, free of that 'Will they stop me?' angst common in many countries. Customs in Poland is basically a formality. If you come from a non-EU country you are allowed 250 duty-free purchased cigarettes and two litres of alcohol, but much more if your goods have been purchased at a non-duty-free in an EU country.

Accommodation

There are hundreds of hotels, pensions, apartments and individual rooms ranging as always from the less than sublime to the gold card ridiculous. You can reserve a room on the web before you leave home, but once in Poland you won't have to go far to find something to your taste. One factor to take into account is whether your room is facing onto a traffic-noisy or pub-hectic street. If there is an inwards facing courtyard, opt for a room here. Kazimierz is the most atmospheric area of Kraków, with its little hotels and restaurants. Off season, always ask if there is a possibility of a discount; it is common practice in Poland especially at weekends in the cities when business guests are fewer. Continental breakfast – coffee, cheese, cold meats and breads – is normally included in the price. There is plenty of good backpacker accommodation in Poland.

Eating Out
This is great fun in Poland as you will be able to sample such delights as boar and venison and some lovely fish, particularly at the coast and lake district. There are restau-

rants, pavement cafés, hole-in-the-wall establishments, takeaways and ice-cream parlours all over Kraków and the larger Polish cities, and pubs with a good range of live music. Pubs don't always have pub-grub as in UK but do have something that is called 'toast' – in fact, toasted cheese and gherkins, a meal in itself. Look out for queues for open roll meat takeaways. There are Argentinian, Japanese, Chinese, Indian, American (burgers), Lithuanian, Russian, Brazilian and French restaurants, and every different type of combination in between.

Smoking
Everyone seems to puff away in Poland, although hotels and restaurants have been introducing more smoking regulations. Cigarettes can be bought at corner kiosks (where you buy public transport tickets) and they are much cheaper than for example in the UK – a fifth of the price.

Opening Hours
Most shops are open 10:00–18:00 on weekdays although food stores tend to open much earlier but close mid-afternoon. Saturday shut-down is 14:00 or 15:00 and, although most people go to church, these days lots of shops are open on Sundays, especially in the cities. Museums and historic venues are inevitably closed on Mondays and for the rest of the week by 16:00. The most visited churches are usually open from early morning (for Mass) until mid-evening but the less known are grilled off at the entrance porch except for early morning and evening Mass. As an approximate guide, here are some general times:
Offices are generally open Monday–Friday 09:00–17:00.
Shops open Monday–Friday 09:00–18:00, Saturday 10:00–15:00.
Restaurants open daily 11:00–23:00, but close earlier in the country.
Attractions are generally open 09:00–18:00.
Museums, however, are often closed on Mondays.

Time
Poland uses the 24-hour clock. Polish Standard Time is one hour ahead of GMT and six hours ahead of Eastern Standard Time. Daylight Saving Time involves putting your watch back one hour at 03:00 on the last Sunday in October, and one hour

CONVERSION CHART		
FROM	**TO**	**MULTIPLY BY**
Millimetres	Inches	0.0394
Metres	Yards	1.0936
Metres	Feet	3.281
Kilometres	Miles	0.6214
Square kilometres	Square miles	0.386
Hectares	Acres	2.471
Litres	Pints	1.760
Kilograms	Pounds	2.205
Tonnes	Tons	0.984

To convert Celsius to Fahrenheit: x 9 ÷ 5 + 32

PUBLIC HOLIDAYS

1 January • New Year's Day
March/April • Easter Sunday and Easter Monday
1 May • State Holiday
3 May • Constitution Day
May/June • Corpus Christi
15 August • Assumption Feast Day
1 November • All Saints' Day
11 November • National Independence Day
25 December • First Day of Christmas
26 December • Second Day of Christmas

forward at 02:00 on the last Sunday in March.

Communications

Telephones: The international dialing code for Poland is 48. Area codes: Gdańsk (058), Kraków (012), Lublin (081), Mikolajki (087), Olsztyn (089), Poznań (061), Suwałki/Lake Wigry (087), Toruń (056), Warsaw (022), Zakopane (018). When making telephone calls, use the area code (e.g. Kraków 012) within the particular town and also to other places in Poland.

Phone cards can be purchased at any newsstand or kiosk. It is probably best to use a Polish SIM card with your mobile phone. There are many Internet cafés. A free Internet e-mail address can be obtained by contacting www.yahoo.com or www.hotmail.com

Public Call Boxes: These are card-operated and cards are available from newsagents/tobacco street kiosks. The call boxes are multilingual (in fact six languages) and can be found anywhere you see the yellow (*Telekommunikacja Polska*) phones.

Postal Services: Post offices (*Poczta*) are usually open 07:00–19:00 Mon–Fri, some on Sat mornings. Kraków's main post office is at the corner of Westerplatte and Wiepole Streets. There is a computerized queue system. Some newsagents also sell stamps. Courier Service (e.g. DHL) is very expensive in Poland.

Electricity

The current in Poland is 220 volts, 50 Cycles AC. The plugs in Poland are similar to those in most of Europe, usually two-point. But if you have non-European electrical appliances, shavers, hair-dryers, etc., its probably best to carry an adaptor.

Weights and Measures

Poland uses the metric system.

Personal Safety

The only problem you may meet is a rowdy bunch of young drinking tourists from the UK, sampling the delights of inexpensive beer. Kraków is a very safe city but Nowa Huta suburb, built in Soviet times, and Planty Park are a touch dubious at night. There are some pickpockets working crowded trams and buses.

They tend to operate in teams but, because of the nature of their silent trade, they are not violent. You will often see women walking alone at night and there is a general ambience of safety and security. Wearing a money-belt immediately identifies you as a foreigner anywhere in the world. Rather use an inside zip-up pocket. Carry a photo-copy of your passport or ID document with you in case of an accident. The Polish police are armed but seldom use their weapons. However, you will hear their cars wailing and racing around in the cities from time to time.

Medical Emergencies

Ambulance: 999, or 112 from a mobile phone. (But it is highly unlikely that you will be understood in English.) There are **24-hour pharmacies** (*Apteka*). Bring along your empty container for a repeat prescription.
The **Public Health Service** needs much improvement.
Private 24-hour clinics are best, in terms of competence and ability to speak English.

Road Signs

The usual international road signs are used throughout Poland. Warsaw's traffic can build up to fairly awesome proportions in the city centre, but far less so in Kraków and the other cities. Traffic behind a tram has to stop when it does, to allow passengers to get off. Jay walking is part of the scene in Poland but do

GOOD READING

Keneally, Thomas (2000) *Schindler's List*, Scribner. How one man saved 1000 Jews from extermination.
Iwanski, Zbigniew (2007) *The Legends of Cracow*, Wydawnictwo Wam. Beautifully illustrated and marvellous for children.
Partyka, Josef (1992) *Ojcowski National Park*, booklet published by the park. Lovely forests,walks and castles near Kraków.
Burford, Tim, *Hiking guide to Poland and the Ukraine*. Out of print but available in second-hand shops.
Michalec, Boguslaw (2007) *Cracow*, Wydawnictwo

Pascal. Unusual and exuberant guide with fascinating anecdotes and tidbits.
Levi, Primo (2006) *If This is a Man/The Truce*, Abacus. Powerful forgiving biography of an Auschwitz prisoner.
Tokarczuk, Olga (2003) *House of Day, House of Night*. Award-winning modern novel.
Uris, Leon (1983) *Mila 18*. Novel set in the Warsaw ghetto uprising.
Trzciński, Andrzej (2005) *Jewish Heritage. Landmarks and Traces of Jewish culture in Lublin*. Rediscover 'The Magic City', an all but destroyed civilization.

not try to copy the Poles until you know your way around. You drive on the right in Poland and the lack of a Metro in e.g. Kraków can lead to serious traffic jams. Sometimes the rather narrow inter-city roads with lots of blind spots are your only option, and although these are not always good, they are steadily being improved.

Language
Polish is not an easy language for English-speakers but its cadences and rythmns can be very attractive. In the visitor areas and cities English is often spoken, much less so in country areas. Hotel staff nearly always speak some English. German is common and the older generation sometimes understand Russian.

Special Interest Groups
Female Travellers: Women should experience no problems. Kraków is particularly safe. Polish women often walk alone at night and do not hesitate to enter a pub alone.
Travellers with disabilities: Trams with wheelchair lifts and sidewalks with ramps are few and far between. Some pedestrian crossings have a sound message for the blind. The main railway stations in Warsaw and Kraków are well equipped, as are the main post offices. Wheelchair progress along Poland's city pavements can be tricky as cars tend to park half on the sometimes rough pavements. The people are always helpful at these times. Some but not all museums and churches cater for disabled folk.

Gay and Lesbian Travellers: Homosexuality is legal with no Third World hang-ups. But it is still looked upon with a degree of wariness in Catholic Poland. Best to avoid open displays of affection. Warsaw, Kraków and Gdańsk tend to be more tolerant and there are clubs in each.
Children: Poland is exceptionally child-friendly and you will often see dads pushing prams. Children under eight seldom pay when an extra bed is needed in your hotel room. There are high chairs and children's portions in restaurants. Baby-sitting facilities are rare, but available. In Kraków, the Dragon's Lair on Wawel hill is a great place for children, as are the old historical market squares (pre-bedtime exercise) in every city.
Student Travellers: Discounts are available at hostels on presentation of an International Student Card, and youth hostels are now mainly open to all comers. Many other hotels offer discounts.

Etiquette
Poland is a country with a long history of being invaded. Consequently the Poles are quiet, reserved and proud. All this melts into smiles and helpful suggestions once you show willing over a glass of vodka. Wear what you like but be reasonably dress-respectful and camera-wary in churches especially during services. You will find people helpful even when their English is non-existent.

INDEX